Memoirs of Bronzeville

By

Robert Brazil

authorHOUSE™

1663 LIBERTY DRIVE, SUITE 200
BLOOMINGTON, INDIANA 47403
(800) 839-8640
WWW.AUTHORHOUSE.COM

© 2004 Robert Brazil.
All Rights Reserved.

No part of this book may be reproduced, stored in a retrieval system, or transmitted by any means without the written permission of the author.

First published by AuthorHouse 10/23/04

ISBN: 1-4208-0656-4 (e)
ISBN: 1-4208-0657-2 (sc)

Printed in the United States of America
Bloomington, Indiana

This book is printed on acid-free paper.

TABLE OF CONTENTS

CHAPTER ONE THE NEIGHBORHOOD 1

CHAPTER TWO RAYMOND SCHOOL 29

CHAPTER THREE SOCIAL LIFE IN THE NEIGHBORHOOD AND CHICAGO 39

CHAPTER FOUR PHILLIPS HIGH SCHOOL 43

CHAPTER FIVE MATRICULATION TO A HIGHER EDUCATION AND INTEGRATION 55

CHAPTER SIX HISTORICAL BACKGOUND 63

THE RESURRECTION OF BRONZEVILLE 77

NOTES 85

**Figure 1
Newsboy selling the Chicago Defender,
a leading Negro newspaper.
Jack Delano, April, 1942. p.131
Stange, Maren [2003] Bronzeville: Black Chicago in Pictures: New York :The New Press.**

"LADY, LADY WITH THE BALD HEADED BABY, STICK YOUR HEAD OUT THE WINDOW, AND GET THE CHICAGO DEFENDER",

"CHICAGO DEFENDER"

This refrain was heard every Friday morning at sunrise in our neighborhood, sometimes called the Bottoms, the Gap, the Black Belt, and Bronzeville

CHAPTER ONE

THE NEIGHBORHOOD

Figure 2
The Corner Of 35th At Prairie Avenue 2003

My neighborhood was bounded by what is now Interstate 94 to the west, 26th street to the north, 67th street south, and Lake Michigan to the west. I lived at 3508 South Prairie in a six flat on the third floor, and attended Raymond Elementary and Wendell Phillips High Schools. This was my world until I extended it to take the State Street Bus or the "EL" Downtown, where we were only allowed into Goldblatts, The Fair, and Sears to shop. Carson Pirie Scott and Marshall Fields were off limits. If you purchased shoes at the Fair, your foot was x-rayed to determine if the shoe fit. My friends, recent arrivals from the south, told me that Blacks were not allowed to try on their shoes, and they had to be bought by a " best guess". The neighborhood was structured this way because of restrictive covenants agreed upon by realtors, politicians, and landlords.

The Bronzeville area was developed during the first decades of the 20th century, this "city-within-a-city" was home to numerous nationally prominent, African-American-owned and operated businesses and cultural institutions. This district offered a commercial alternative to the race restrictions and indifference that characterized much of the city during the early part of the 20th century. Between 1910 and 1920, during the peak of the "Great Migration," the population of the area increased dramatically when thousands of African-Americans fled the oppression of the south and emigrated to Chicago in search of industrial jobs. Further development of the area was halted by the onset of the Great Depression. Many famous people were associated with the development of the area including: Jesse Biga, banker ; Anthony Overton, entrepreneur; Joseph Jordan, musician; Andrew "Rube" Foster, founder of the Negro National Baseball League; Ida B. Wells, a civil rights activist, journalist and organizer of the NAACP; Bessie Coleman, the first African-American woman pilot; and Louis Armstrong, the legendary trumpet player and bandleader who performed at many of the area's night clubs. The name, "Black Metropolis," became firmly established with the publication of a 1945 sociological study of the same title, In later years the area was referred to as "Bronzeville," a term attributed to an editor at the Chicago Bee.

1. Copyright 2003 City of Chicago Department of Planning and Development, Landmarks Division http://www.ci.chi.il.us/landmarks/B/BlackMet.html

Mrs. Alfreda Duster, Daughter of Ida B. Wells-Barnett, was my mentor for much of my formative years. I was her paperboy, and a willing victim to her never ending stories about our heritage, and why we should be proud. She was instrumental in my attending Camp Illini, in Marseilles, Illinois, serving as a counselor at the camp, and micro managing my education outside of the formal education in schools. Her son, Troy Duster, PhD. Graduated from Wendell Phillips High School, as Valedictorian in 1953. Dr. Donald Smith, informed me that Troy is head of the Psychology Department at New York University. My sister, Mrs. Vera Green, retired principal, 2003, of the Green Elementary School, graduated in this same class. Mrs Duster introduced me to many famous people of renown, but I'll only mention two of them: General Benjamin O. Davis, Jr., and Former Governor of Illinois, William G. Stratton. Both were introduced, and held long conversations with me, while I was camp Counselor at Camp Illini, Marseilles, Illinois.

Ida B. Wells-Barnett was one of the leading civil rights crusaders at the turn of the century. She was educated at Rust University, a high school and industrial school for freedmen established in Holly Springs in 1866. After the death of her parents and three siblings in a yellow fever epidemic, she began teaching. She bought a one-third interest in *The Free Speech and Headlight*, a black newspaper in Memphis, and began a career as an investigative reporter, specializing in cases of civil rights violations against black Americans. In 1895, she published "The Red Record," a study on lynchings which concluded that race hatred, not rape, was the real reason behind the rising number of lynchings of African Americans. She went on to mount a powerful crusade against lynchings. She married Ferdinand Lee Barnett, the founder of the *Conservator*, the first black-owned newspaper in Chicago. After settling in Chicago in 1895, Wells worked as a probation officer, a woman's club organizer, and the founder and director of the Negro Fellowship League, which provided assistance to homeless young black men. In honor of he work in Chicago, a housing project in Chicago was named after her in 1940. 2.www.chipub.org/001hwcl/gisnotableafam.html

In 1940, William G. Stratton was elected U.S.

Congressman-at-large   at 25 years of age, becoming the

youngest member in the nation of the U.S. House of Representatives and was known as the "Baby of the House"; in 1942 he became the youngest constitutional officer in the State of Illinois when he was elected State treasurer; in 1948 he lost his bid for the position of Secretary of State, and joined the United States Navy, serving as lieutenant in the South Pacific during World War II.

Mr. Stratton regained his seat in the U.S. House; in 1950 he reclaimed the State treasurer's office; in 1952 he defeated Lieutenant Governor Sherwood Dixon to win the gubernatorial election, and he was elected to a second term as Governor.

William Stratton spoke out against racial discrimination, attempted to create a fair- employment commission, and named the first woman and first African American woman to a gubernatorial cabinet. 3.http://www.legis.state.il.us/legislation/legisnet92/hrgroups/hr/920hr0113LV.html

Robert Brazil

GENERAL BENJAMIN O. DAVIS, JR.

Lieutenant General Benjamin Oliver Davis Jr., is deputy commander in chief, U.S. Strike Command with headquarters at MacDill Air Force Base, Fla. He had additional duty as deputy U.S. commander in chief, Middle-East, Southern Asia and Africa. General Davis was born in Washington, 5.C., in 1912. He graduated from Central High School in Cleveland, Ohio, in 1929, attended Western Reserve University at Cleveland and later the University of Chicago. He entered the U.S. Military Academy at West Point, N.Y., in July 1932 and graduated in June 1936 with a commission as a second lieutenant of infantry. In June 1937 after a year as commander of an infantry company at Fort Benning, Ga., he entered the Infantry School there and a year later graduated and assumed duties as professor of military science at Tuskegee Institute, Tuskegee, Ala. In May 1941 he entered Advanced Flying School at nearby Tuskegee Army Air Base and received his pilot wings in March 1942.

General Davis transferred to the Army Air Corps in May 1942. As commander of the 99th Fighter Squadron at Tuskegee Army Air Base, he moved with his unit to North Africa in April 1943 and later to Sicily. He returned to the United States in October 1943, assumed command of the 332d Fighter Group at Selfridge Field, Mich., and returned with the group to Italy two months later. In 1949 General Davis went to the Air War College, Maxwell Air Force Base, Ala.; and after graduation, he was assigned to the Deputy Chief of Staff for Operations, Headquarters U.S. Air Force, Washington, D.C. He served in various capacities with the headquarters until July 1953, when he went to the advanced jet fighter gunnery school at Nellis Air Force Base, Nev. His military decorations include the Air Force Distinguished Service Medal, Army Distinguished Service Medal, Silver Star, Legion of Merit with two oak leaf clusters, Distinguished Flying Cross, Air Medal with four oak leaf clusters, Air Force Commendation Medal with two oak leaf clusters and the Philippine Legion of Honor. He is a command pilot.

4.http://www.af.mil/bios/bio_5173.shtml

Travel through the neighborhood was primarily by "bus". The Chicago Motor Coach company had buses that ran on the boulevards, and the Chicago Transit Company covered the other streets. The Chicago Transit Company bought out the Chicago Motor Coach Company, and prices have risen steadily since. The other mode of transportation in the neighborhood was by "jitney", or unlicensed taxis. They initially ran north and south on Indiana Avenue, and later, South Parkway. I had no idea that they were illegal, because there were so many of them. The fare was 15 cents, but it cost more if you wanted the driver to leave his route, and take you to a nearby street.

I took pictures of my neighborhood and like all urban areas, it has changed dramatically. On either side of 35th street, between Indiana Avenue, and South Parkway, [Martin Luther King, Jr., Drive], there was one mom and pop business, after another, That business supported that family. Closer to my home, on the south side of 35th Street, there was a drug store on the southeast corner of Indiana Avenue, and eastward, a live chicken house, where you selected your chicken, and they cut off the head, and defeathered the chicken while you waited. This establishment was next to Al and Harry's poolroom and bar, a "chicken in the box" restaurant, a beauty parlor, a store that cleaned and blocked hats, south of the drugstore on Indiana, a cigar store on the southwest corner of 35th at Indiana,, Smitty's Corner on the northwest corner, Jay's Men's Store on the northeast corner. Pekins Cleaners occupied the southeast corner of 35th at Prairie, with grocery stores on the other three corners of 35th at Prairie. Between Indiana and Prairie, there was also a take-out restaurant, that sold fried fish. The fish restaurant, and" chicken in the box" restaurants, were always filled to capacity, with party-goers on their way home at two or three o'clock in the morning. A Mc Donalds and larger business establishments presently occupy the entire south side of 35th street, replacing my six flat home, grocery stores, and all of the businesses between Indiana and Prairie. I fondly remember an ice cream parlor on the north side of 35th Street between Prairie and Giles Avenues.

In the Autobiography of Malcolm X, Malcolm X noted that whenever a "black leader", was interviewed on television, he always seemed to look back in time to remember that professional blacks were the role models for black people, and that they have been replaced by professional athletes, and drug dealers. It is probably difficult to imagine for today's youth, but I remember when there were no black baseball players, basketball players, or football players to idolize. I remember Jackie Robinson, and Larry Doby, entering the National and American Leagues with the Brooklyn Dodgers, and Cleveland Indians, respectively. I played against Sweetwater Clifton as a softball player in Chicago. He was the first to play professional basketball that I could remember. He batted left-handed, and could hit the 16" softball a country mile. Malcolm X felt that integration, or how it was implemented, had injured the black community, and would cause further divisions, instead of having blacks come together. Indeed, many of my colleagues feel that blacks have a " crabs in the barrel mentality", or the "first or only black to do this or that" mentality.

Figure 3
The Victory Monument Memorial To Black Soldiers In World War One

This scene is especially memorable because it contains much of the history of Bronzeville in one snapshot. In the foreground is the "War Memorial for Black Soldiers", and behind it are the closed doors of Supreme liberty Life Insurance Company, on the corner of 35th at King Drive. In the background are The Lake Meadows Apartments. Lake Meadows and Prairie Shores Apartments replaced large mansions inhabited by black professionals. As an elementary school student, I delivered newspapers for the now defunct " Chicago Daily News". I remember delivering the newspapers, as the mansions were being destroyed, to be replaced by Lake Meadows. I wondered how many of us would remember the power and impact of a residential section of mansions, similar to the mansions in Kenwood, and Jackson Park Highlands on Chicago's south side.

Victory Monument

Address: 35th Street and King Drive Year Built: 1926

Architect: John A. Nyden

Date Designated a Chicago Landmark: September 9, 1998. This structure was erected to honor the meritorious achievements of the Eighth Regiment of the Illinois National Guard, an African-American unit that served in France during World War I as part of the 370th U.S. Infantry (also see Eighth Regiment Armory). The bronze panels and the soldier atop the monument, which was added in 1936, were designed by Leonard Crunelle, a former pupil of noted Chicago sculptor Lorado Taft. The monument was dedicated on Armistice Day (November 11th) in 1928. It is the site of an annual Memorial Day ceremony and is one of nine structures in the Black Metropolis-Bronzeville Historic District.

5. Copyright 2003 City of Chicago Department of Planning and Development, Landmarks Division. http://www.ci.chi.il.us/Landmarks/V/Victory.html

Figure 4.
Lake Meadows Apartments

Lake Meadows is an affordable 22 story luxury apartment building that prides itself on location and service. Lake Michigan is practically next door and the downtown Loop is just a few blocks away. The best of Chicago is around every turn... Entertainment, restaurants, shopping, museums, transportation, theaters and much more. At Lake Meadows they not only offer you the convenience of location but also the luxury of services and comfort. All this and at affordable prices. Lake Meadows is truly one of the best that Chicago has to offer.

Supreme Life Building
Address: 3501 S. King Dr.
Year Built: 1921 (remodeled 1950)
Architect: Albert Anis
Date Designated a Chicago Landmark:
September 9, 1998

This was the longtime headquarters of the first African-American owned and operated insurance company in the northern United States. Founded in 1919 by Frank L. Gillespie (as the Liberty Life Insurance Company), the firm moved in 1921 into the second floor of this building, which had been constructed by the Roosevelt State Bank. Liberty Life bought the entire structure in 1924 and, in 1929, merged with two out-of-state firms to form the Supreme Life Insurance Company of America. In 1950, after becoming one of the few major businesses of "Black Metropolis" to survive the Great Depression, the company modernized the building by covering the original classical-style facade with porcelain-metal panels.

6. Black Metropolis-Bronzeville Historic District. Copyright 2003 City of Chicago Department of Planning and Development, Landmarks Division

http://www.ci.chi.il.us/Landmarks/S/Supreme.html

EARL B. DICKERSON

Earl B. Dickerson was a fraternity brother in Kappa Alpha Psi. He was one of the founders of Beta Chapter, University of Illinois, Champaign-Urbana. He was instrumental in the founding and development of Supreme Liberty Life Insurance Company. Mr. Dickerson never was at a loss for words, when sharing black history lessons, with those of us who were, and are less informed.

Earl B. Dickerson was known as "the dean of Chicago's black lawyers,". Mr. Dickerson was also a Chicago alderman. He helped organize the NAACP Legal Defense and Educator Fund in 1939. Born in Mississippi, Dickerson moved to Chicago when he was 15. His mother bribed railroad porters to hide her son aboard a train to escape racial oppression in the South. A graduate of the University of Illinois in 1914, he taught for a year at Tuskegee University in Alabama. He completed a law degree at the University of Chicago Law School in 1920. He became the first general counsel o the Supreme Life Insurance Co. of America, one of the largest black-owned insurance companies. He later became the company's president and chairman of the board. In 1939, Dickerson ran against William L. Dawson for the 2nd Ward aldermanic seat and won. He served on the City Council from 1939-1943. In 1930 he represented the father of Chicago playwright Lorraine Hansberry in the case o Hansberry vs. Lee, successfully argued before the Supreme Court for an end to restrictive real-estate covenant.

7. http://www.chipublib.org/001hwlc/gisnotableafam.html

Robert Brazil

Figure 5.
People shopping for shoes on Maxwell Street, Russell Lee, April, 1941.
p.101.
Stange, Maren [2003] Bronzeville: Black Chicago in Pictures, 1941-1943.
New York: The New Press

THE MAXWELL STREET SHOPPING CENTER ON 12TH STREET AT HALSTED THE CENTER WAS MOVED TO CANAL STREET TO MAKE ROOM FOR THE UNIVERSITY OF ILLINOIS AT CHICAGO EXPANSION

I earned about $12.00 weekly as a paperboy. My parents would not allow me to deliver newspapers in the morning, or during the coldest winter months. I worked for the Chicago Daily News, because they were an afternoon newspaper, and allowed me to work after school, without interfering with my studies. Because, I was independent, and wanted to support myself as much as I could, I purchased most of my clothing from the Maxwell Street Market on the west side of Chicago. One of the favorite stores was "Smoky Joes". The clothing was cheap, looked good, and lasted a season. The only thing that I didn't like about "Smoky Joes" were the bright yellow bags that they placed your clothes in. They were so loud that your fellows could not only see you coming, they could also hear you.

When I left to attend elementary, and secondary school, I remember seeing blacks in white shirts, suits, and ties, and well dressed women, as well as laborers, going to work. I remember a man who purchased a Cadillac almost every year, giving my friends and me, softball equipment to clean up the glass in the alleys. I remember seeing teachers, attorneys, and other professionals leaving for their respectable employment. My sister, Vera, taught, and received a Masters degree from Loyola University before we moved from 35th Street to Chatham. She was one of the first black math consultants, and retired as a school principal in 2003, after 45 years in the Chicago school system. My younger sister, Elaine, was a State Scholar, professional artist, Midwest Representative for the Black Students Union, and was instrumental in bringing the "Black House" to Northwestern University, from where she graduated , before moving on to Cornell University. Role models were not in short supply for me or any other young men or women, who lived in the "Black Belt". I remember one of my classmates from Raymond Elementary School proudly sharing the news that seven of us had received doctorate degrees from established universities. I saw the unfairness of "redlining" by the realtors, when we high school students attended football games,at Eckersall Stadium on 82nd at Yates Boulevard. I wondered why we couldn't purchase a house and live in a marvelous neighborhood like this one. I taught for five years after graduating from college, and was assigned to Tesla Elementary School as an Assistant Principal. I purchased a home at 8200 South Yates Boulevard, across the street from Eckersall Stadium. I was the second black to move into the neighborhood which changed from primarily "jewish" to "black", almost overnight. I remember cutting the grass in my front yard, and sighted a colleague from college. I waved, and she ignored me. I think that she thought that I was working in the landscaping business. She returned a week later, and was very friendly. I think that someone must have told her that I was the owner of the house, not a yardman for a "white owner".

THROWING ROCKS AT THE TRAIN

My first experience with the police was in fact very friendly. There was a Police Station near 35th and Rhodes called the Stanton Avenue Police Station. I don't know why, since there was no Stanton Avenue that I knew about anywhere in the neighborhood. The police in the station would allow pre-teen boys into the station for casual discussions until the Sergeants would chase us out. This was the professional home of " Officer Frazier", a singular black police youth officer who was responsible for keeping all neighborhood youth in line. He seemed to be everywhere. I was walking in a neighborhood with two friends, Snookie Williams and Elliott Ford, when we decided to throw rocks at passing trains. We were captured by police officers within ten minutes, taken home for the traditional "whipping" and told to report to the Stanton Avenue Police Station every Saturday for the remainder of the summer. That's when I officially met Officer Frazier. Our initiation into his club was to line up all of the boys who had been arrested before us and send us through a " beltline". It wasn't so bad and you healed within a week." Officer Frazier" was a one man police force for kids. The police officer responsible for adults was "Two-Gun Pete". We never met.

There was an unwritten rule in the neighborhood that after school, you would come home, take off your school clothes, and change into your "play clothes", or "rain clothes". I was playing in a sand box with one of my friends, J.C. and we were wearing the same type of caps. He had not changed into his playclothes, and someone must have called my house. My grandmother came out and snatched J.C. out of the sandbox, and proceeded to give him a quick whipping which was common in the neighborhood, and could be administered by any neighbor if the parents were at work, or "not available ". They would then tell your parents, who gave you a "follow up whipping" for disturbing the neighborhood. J.C. asked me why I didn't stop her. I told him that I was surprised and frozen with fear. I didn't tell him that she had poor eyesight and couldn't tell us apart.

GANGS IN THE NEIGHBORHOOD

I had heard about gangs in the neighborhood, but it did not mean much to me until one day I was sitting on the stairway at the building next to my house with my pre-teen friends listening to the teen age boys telling lies on each other. A large group of teen-agers came out of nowhere shooting at my friends with single shot homemade guns, called in fact, home-mades. My friends took off as one, and the outsiders didn't catch or shoot anybody, but it was extremely frightening to witness this harrowing experience at such close quarters.

I remember Charles Townsend, who I believe is serving life in prison for murdering and robbing four men, testing his home made guns, by shooting them against a brick wall. The police arrived and almost caught Charles. To the children in the neighborhood, Charles was not a bad fellow. Every now and then, he would steal a bakery truck, and give away all the goods to the neighborhood kids. His brother, Tuck, was one of my best friends.

The immediate gangs, social clubs, softball teams, in my neighborhood, were the Leprecons, Deacons, Giles A.C.'s, Vagabonds, the 34th Street Boys, and the Valiant Men. There were others, but I'm not as familiar with them. The Blackstone Rangers, later the El Rukins, the Disciples, Latin Kings, and Simon City Royals came later.

Almost everyone wears sunglasses today. It is a huge industry. During my pre-teen and teen years, only the coolest boys wore sunglasses. There were several styles in vogue: The boys in my club, the Gentlemen, and the Conservatives wore ivy league clothes; v-necked cashmere or wool sweaters, leather jackets, and khaki pants. The "Gausters" wore marcel or chemically controlled hair, like the "tango dancers in movies". The "big hat boys" were the coolest. They wore broad brimmed hats, long overcoats, and sunglasses, inside and outdoors. If you called one on the telephone, the likely response would be " I mean Hello", and if you called their name on the street, it took forever for them to turn around, and acknowledge you. They went to the "Peps", to do "the walk", a mid-style dance between the "two step" and the "bop". I never made it to the Peps. It closed before I was old enough to go.

One night, my brother, James, and his friends were leaving " The Peps", when they noticed a fight taking place down the street. The winner in the fight was beating his opponent with his overcoat thrown over his head so that you couldn't see who the victim was. They had been searching for Greg Jackson, whose parents owned the school store, where I stopped every day on my way to Raymond School. Greg was handsome, had a gift for gab, was a ladies man, and he talked too much. I loved his personality, because he always gave me special attention , in the poolroom. When the fight was over, and they still couldn't find Greg, they walked over, and removed the coat from the victim, and of course, it was Greg.

The neighborhood at the Oakland Square was famous long before the El Rukins occupied the theatre as a gang headquarters. I worked at the Oakland Square Theatre during my Junior and Senior years in high school. I would attend school, go to football practice, go to the theatre, work as an usher, and I sometimes took tickets at the door. The box office would close at 10:00pm and I would study at the theatre door until closing, close to midnight.

The neighborhood was famous for its' prostitutes. Every hotel, headed by the famous Du Sable Hotel, catered to every taste. If you wanted a woman with green hair, she would appear shortly with green hair, dripping wet. The pimps brought their favorites to the theatre, and I got to know them, but I kept my distance.

Neighbors always had a responsibility to tell your parents if you had been a "bad boy". I came home one day after doing everything that I was big enough to do, and my mother was on the telephone talking to several neighbors on the "party line". She turned and looked at me, and whispered, "Lord, don't make me a murderer". I couldn't determine who she was talking about since I was the only other person in the room.

Al and Harry's was located on 35th Street between Prairie and Indiana. It was a bar and poolroom. I was not allowed in there. Harry ran out to stop a fight one day and was stabbed to death. They simply drew a line through his name and the new name was "Al's".

One of our friends, a good fellow named Mervin was in a fight alongside William Pritchett's house. He had Pritchett to hold his groceries while he fought. Midway through the fight, he kept yelling for Pritchett to give him his groceries. We thought that he was going to throw them at his opponent. When Pritchett handed him the groceries, he turned and fled directly home.

One of the known quantities about living in the hood was, if you partied all night, you still had to go to Sunday School and Church, or at least to Church on Sunday. One of the girls who attended Phillips High school with us came out early to receive her Sunday newspaper. She saw William Pritchett dragging himself into his home located on the first floor. She feared that he was close to death, but when she arrived at St. Lukes Baptist Church later that day, she said that what she saw amazed her. We were in the front row singing louder than anybody else. We had reserved seating in the front row because when no sinner would step forward to be "saved", at Reverend Grayson's urging, we were handy to have around. I can't count the number of times that we were saved.

The only other time that I was amazed was when the regular Pastor, Reverend Sanders, of Mt. Aaron Baptist Church was not able to preach. He was replaced by an Assistant Pastor. It was a Wednesday night service, and my mother had to force us to go. The Assistant Pastor, however, was in a soul saving mood. The entire "Amen Section" of the Deacon Board was rocking to his message of "fire and brimstone". The next thing that happened I'll never forget. The minister ran across the top of ten pews to the right of the pulpit and started preaching from the window. We were frozen in time. He then preached for about fifteen minutes and again ran across the tops of the pews to return to the pulpit. The next month when this was again on the schedule, my mother had no trouble getting us ready. We kept yelling for her to hurry up. You could imagine our disappointment when Reverend Sanders returned to restore a civilized sermon from the pulpit.

Figure 6.
Bronzeville: Black Chicago in Pictures, 1941-1943:
In front of the Pilgrim Baptist Church
on Easter Sunday. Russell Lee, April, 1941. p. 180.
Stange, Maren [2003] Bronzeville: Black Chicago in Pictures,1941-1943.New York: The New Press

"My brother, James, attended Pilgrims Baptist Church every Sunday without fail"

Icing Green, "The Banana King", weighed and sold bananas from the back of a "pick-up Truck. One of our favorite hobbies was to ride by on our bicycles and snatch a banana from his truck. But don't get the wrong idea. When Icing Green needed workers, he recruited us to work on a Saturday, weighing and selling his bananas from the back of the truck. We were very efficient, we were good counters and well schooled in the art of pleasing adult women. Most of us acquired this skill from simply living in a neighborhood where black women were queens, and seemingly had the power of " life and death" over us. When a "mother" got off the bus, from "cleaning house", or doing "piece work", she would normally have to carry groceries from Krogers, or another "white owned store". She never had to worry about carrying them all the way home. We would take the groceries, inquired about her "weight loss", and explained to her what a pleasure it was to assist. I don't know of any boy in the neighborhood who didn't have this verbal delivery "down pat"[a common expression]. We knew that this woman would be on the phone to our mothers to tell her what " well behaved children" we were. We called it "making points". The other area that assisted us in developing "people skills" was going to the "A and P", across the street from Phillips High School, with our wagons. We carried groceries home for tips, and normally earned about $5.00 in four hours.

SPORTS IN THE NEIGHBORHOOD

GIRLS SOFTBALL TEAMS

The girls in my neighborhood were extremely talented softball players. They had teams and they walked to other neighborhoods to challenge other teams. There were at least one hundred of us who walked with them and watched the games.

IN EVERY NEIGHBORHOOD, YOU COULD DRIVE BY AND WATCH SOFTBALL GAMES BETWEEN GOOD TEAMS

The Wabash YMCA summer softball tournament was the biggest thing other than the Madden Park and Washington Park softball tournaments. I was thrilled because at age 10, I played second base with the 12-14 year old boys on the Intermediate teams, instead of the 10-12 Junior teams. My team was the Leprecons. It took us two summers to dethrone the "Tigers", who lived around the Wabash YMCA. They defended their turf as though their lives depended on it.

My most important moment in sports came at the Pontiac Lot on 33rd and Prairie when I hit a double with the bases loaded against the "Dons", one of the neighborhood top teams. That hit won the game for the Leprecons.

Figure 7.
The Wabash Ymca

An important center of community life, this Young Men's Christian Association facility also provided housing and job training for new arrivals from the South during the "Great Migration" of African-Americans in the first decades of the 20th century. A notable aspect of the buildings diverse history was the founding here, in 1915, of the Association for the Study of Negro Life and History, one of the first groups devoted to African-American studies. The building was expanded to the south in 1945. It closed as a YMCA in the late 1970's. It is one of nine structures in the <u>Black Metropolis-Bronzeville Historic District.</u>

8. Copyright 2003 City of Chicago Department of Planning and Development, Landmarks Division.

http://www.ci.chi.il.us/LNDMARKS/w/wABASH YMCA.html

If you drove through the south side of Chicago during the summer, you could watch talented softball teams playing with 16" clincher softballs on every vacant lot that would allow a game to be played. Chicago was unique, and we loved it that way.

I played on the Ada S. Mc Kinley Community House softball team with an adult coach and sponsor. It was common in our neighborbood to have black men to tell us what to do. I spent many afternoons on 34th and Michigan. We scheduled games at the Pontiac Lot, 33rd at Prairie, behind Pilgrims Baptist Church, and across the street from Mrs. Alfreda Duster's house. Mrs Duster was Ida B. Wells daughter. I was Mrs. Duster's paperboy. We also played games in the open lot to the east of Comiskey Park. That area was not a safe place to be if you were alone. I'm sure that the Ada S. Community Center, along with the Southside Boys Club, kept us out of a lot of trouble.

figure 8
Ada S. Mc Kinley Community Center On 34th At Michigan Avenue 2003

THE KAPPA ALPHA PSI SOFTBALL TEAMS

The Kappa Alpha Psi, Alumni Chapter Softball Team, was unique because of a man named Dodo Maxfield. Dodo weighed well over three hundred pounds, and cursed every misplay of his team. It was not unusual for Dodo to bet over a thousand dollars on every game. I popped up in the last inning against " The Jive ten Old Men" out of Madden Park once, and Dodo cursed me all the way back to the dugout. I turned on him and yelled. " I'm three for four, and Dodo replied, " yeah, but you SOB, you can't hit in the clutch". Dodo also coached and managed an All American basketball team of Kappas in the Jackson Park Tournament, but that's another story. The softball team was manned by men who became somewhat famous in their own right. Ben Bluitt, later coach of the Detroit University basketball team was the pitcher. Paul Patterson, a former Chicago Bear was the first baseman, I played second base, and later Al Pritchett, my best friend's brother in high school played second base. Al was a state champion trackman out of Phillips High School, and Marquette Universities' first Black football captain when Marquette played football. Harold Pates, who later became President of Kennedy King College, played short center, common only in Chicago 16" softball. The shortstop was Mack Smith, later the Principal of Harlan High School, and the Third baseman was Jim Peoples, later a south suburban Principal and School Superintendent. The left fielder was Chuck Smith, who managed the political campaign of the first black mayor of Gary, Indiana. The center fielder was Wilson " Squint" Frost, a Chicago Alderman, and political insider. The left fielder was Bobby Bates, the highest ranking Black administrator in the United States Postal Service. Everybody played catcher. We just rotated. We tried to enter the Daddy O. Daylie Softball Tournament on 71st and South Parkway, now Dr. Martin Luther King, Jr. Drive. We were barred out for gambling, because we were thought of as professionals. However, other teams were entered who also played for money. They simply changed their names. Dodo also entered us in tournaments with mostly "white teams". The games were played in the lot beside what is now Simeon High School. Dodo gave us a choice of two names, The M----- F-----s, or the Freedom Riders. We chose "Freedom Riders".

The undergraduate softball team was almost as imposing. I was the captain and we played anybody who dared to challenge us. We lost to the Alumni team in a fierce battle in Washington Park 32-19 for two dollars a man. We had difficulty getting games because many of our players played football and enjoyed taking out shortstops and second basemen with cross body blocks. We played at Stateway Gardens, one of the most dangerous projects in the city, and ran one team off before the game was finished. They just grabbed all of the bases and ran. They didn't believe that our team was composed of teachers, principals, police officers, and attorneys. We lost one game to the "Playboys", with hundreds of people watching without incident. Dodo Maxfield bought all of the equipment for the game for both teams. We were skilled and interchangeable, except at third base where Chauncey Bertha, Principal, Sexton School, George Wilson, PE Director of Baseball, Chicago Public Schools, and George Stanton, PE Director of Basketball, Chicago Public Schools, Basketball Coach of 1998 State Basketball Champion, Whitney Young High School, dared anyone to move them. Carl Boyd played shortstop, I played first base because our first baseman, J.P. Malone, the first baseman changed positions with me in left field, because he refused to catch the balls from Carl Boyd's rocket arm. J.W. Smith, City Wide Director of Physical Education, Chicago Public Schools, Willie Saxton, Physical Education Administrator, Chicago Public Schools, Dr. Major Armstead, Sub-District Superintendent, Chicago Public Schools, and Superintendent of Schools, Kenosha, Wisconsin, and the other team members were interchangeable, outstanding athletes, who could play anywhere, and any sport. Lamont Wyche, Phd. University of Illinois, Champaign-Urbana, and Assistant Superintendent, Minneapolis, Minnesota, who played center field, was an outstanding basketball player. He always Yelled " I got it", no matter where the ball was hit.

My three most terrifying experiences happened when I lost two friends, and almost a third. The first was Charles King. Charles was very handsome, and had an identical twin, Richard. When the vacant lot on 35th and Prairie froze over every winter, we would ice skate. We always built a fire close-by to keep warm. Apparently someone, not in our group, had earlier left a bullet on the ground, underneath where our fire was built. The bullet exploded, and wounded Charles. Because he was such a comedian, we did not immediately react. But moments later, when we realized that he was injured, we notified neighbors, who called for the Police, and an ambulance. Charles died on the way to the hospital. Charles and Richard were cousins to the Brakes family. Mr. And Mrs. Brakes had twelve boys before a girl was conceived. All of the boys, except one, attended Phillips High School, where they became track and basketball super stars. The oldest boy, Horace, Jr. was one of my best friends. He attended Dunbar High School, our arch-rival. He grew to 6'9" and became one of the outstanding basketball players in Chicago.

**Figure 9.
The Illinois Central Railroad Tracks At 35th Street**

It was a normal exercise for us to go to the 31st Street Beach by walking east on 35th Street and crossing the bridge. Somehow, on this day, friends of mine decided to become adventurous, and walk across the railroad tracks underneath the bridge. The tracks were electric, but they said that they were careful. One of our smaller and less sophisticated friends, named Mickey, stepped into a track and could not get his foot out. They were not successful before the train arrived, and hit Mickey, killing him. When I think back, it seemed like a simple thing to do, if you only took his foot out of his shoe. I don't remember what happened after that. I do recall the boys coming back to the neighborhood. Anyone could tell that something was wrong. I remember that the boy, who lived in the same building as Mickey, had to break the news to his mother while we waited outside, crying.

The third episode that was most frightening had a happier ending. I was eight years old, and my best friend, and next door neighbor, Kenneth Walls, heard my brother, James, age 16, discussing how he and his friends, were going over to Lake Michigan for a swim. My brother was an excellent swimmer, and he still participates on swim teams in Chicago. The "big boys" told us that we couldn't go. We ignored them and followed them, until we were too far away from home for them to send us back. We were having a wonderful time. The "big boys had supplied us with a rubber raft, and kept a close eye on us. Kenneth, however jumped at the raft, and missed. The undertow must have been terrific. We were looking for him when he emerged ten feet away. My brother jumped in and quickly pulled him to shore, saving his life. We were all sworned to secrecy, because I don't know if any of us would have survived our parents' wrath, if they had ever found out.

The neighborhood theatres were to be attended on Saturday only. We could only attend the Joe Louis Theatre on 35th Street between Michigan and Indiana Avenues. We could attend the others, but only if we went together, and left together in a group. We could not attend the "State" on 35th and State Street, the "Grand", on 31st and State, or the "Ritz", on Oakwood Blvd. [40th Street], and South Parkway, Now Martin Luther King, Jr. Drive, unless we attended together. The Ritz was located around the corner from where Minnie Riperton, and Herbie Hancock lived. Minnie Riperton's sister, Clarice, a real beauty, graduated from high school with me. Herbie Hancock's brother, Wayman, was a fraternity brother, and close friend, who delivered "special delivery" for the U.S. Post Office.

I should mention that all of us worked at the Post Office in December, twelve hours a day, in high school, and all the way through college. We normally worked four hours daily, while attending university classes and twelve hours, during the "Christmas Rush". We called our employment, "Post Office Scholarships".

There were not nearly as many "tackle football" teams in the neighborhood, probably because the equipment was expensive, and if it was not showcased at the Catholic Salvage on 35th and Michigan, it wouldn't be available to us. We, however, put together an excellent football team and challenged the other four or five teams in the neighborhood. We were asked to play a team from 34th and Prairie, which was across 35th street, a gang dividing line. John Scarbrough, the future quarterback of Dunbar High School was our quarterback. When we were nearing the nearing the end of the game and leading 12-0, we noticed that an inordinate number of non-participants had gathered along the sidelines. John Scarbrough announced that this was the last play. He was going to score a touchdown and continue to run through the open gate at the north end of the Pontiac Lot. Anyone who could not score with him was on his own. John scored the touchdown, and continued his run through the gate. The onlookers then noticed that we were not coming back for the kick-off. We had to run south, and past them to get back to our neighborhood. They began climbing the fence, which had barbed wire at the top. When we got to where they were stranded at the top, we stopped, and began to stone them with a passion.

Phillips High School was the center of most of our activities. We played basketball there almost every night of the week. I had two fights after the games that I tried to avoid. Clarence Snyder, manager of the football team, and my close friend, and I were going home and we were stopped, headed by a group led by Lefty Bearden. Eugene Bearden was also a friend, but for some reason, he wanted to fight Clarence Snyder. Clarence was not a fighter, and I explained to "Lefty", that Clarence was with me, and I couldn't allow him to beat up on my friend. Without any further provocation, he attacked me. I won the fight, and we continued on our way.

The second fight was not as quickly won. As a matter of fact, I couldn't say "you should see the other guy", because of the viciousness of the fight. Alfred Bradley's cousin was visiting from somewhere, and remarked to the group, while walking home from the Phillips basketball game, that I had torn a button off of his shirt. I knew that I hadn't, but to appease him, I told him to come home with me and my mother would sew it back on the shirt. He told me that he didn't want my mama to fix it in a very derogatory tone. In our neighborhood, if someone said something about your mother, you had to fight, even if the challenger was King Kong. At the time, I was about 6', and 160 pounds. I had to wait two years to make the Phillips football team, because, when I graduated from Raymond Elementary, I was 4'11", and weighed 100 pounds. My opponent weighed from 180-190 and was a battle scarred veteran, pretty much like me. I wasn't afraid of him, but my mother was another story.

I decided to try to take him out with the first punch. He shook his head, as if loosening up, grabbed me, and threw me over the hood of a car into Indiana Avenue, and passing traffic. He then followed over the hood of the car, and I met him at the top. We must have battled for a long time, because the Penecostal Church on Indiana Avenue emptied, and I heard someone say, "throw some holy water on them". I think the men from Clark's Poolroom came out and eventually stopped this bloodbath. My friends took me inside, washed me off so that I would be presentable when I got home, and my mother would not have to address the situation.

Nick and Angels was the accepted "school Store" across the street from Phillips High School. When I visited Du Sable High, I was surprised that there was a second "Nick and Angel's" there. The store that we were warned about as students and athletes was Ms. Johnson's Bakery, located directly across the street, and south of the high school. Her bakery goods, especially the donuts were fabulous. However, a stomach ache was not uncommon, after downing two or three of her donuts. We referred to her bakery goods as, Ms. Johnson's "belly bruisers".

In my pre-teen years, I was a Chicago White Sox fan, without any money. When the New York Yankees, the Boston Red Sox, or the Cleveland Indians came to town, every kid, black or white lined up outside the fence on 35th Street to jump the fence, and watch the game. We would wait patiently for the game to start, and for the police Lieutenant to make his final inspection. We were not alone. There were at least twenty five Police officers on the other side of the fence, watching us. We gathered there every Tuesday, and Friday night to watch the aforementioned teams. The Police Sargeant would then give us the speech that we knew "by heart", and we recited it along with him. Once the Police Lieutenant was out of sight, he and his gang of twenty five, [my perception, not his] would walk to the end of the stadium. They would catch the last of the offenders, give them a quick belt massage, and put them back outside the gate. Anyone who did not get in had to go home, and " better luck, next time". The key to getting in of course was to be brave and go with the first bunch. I wasn't brave, but, I didn't want a belt massage, and I wanted to see the game. So, I always went with the first group of crazies.

The White Sox had Minnie Minoso, Jim Landis in center, who couldn't hit, but who caught every ball, Chico Carascel at shortstop, Nellie Fox at second, Jim Rivera in right, and a pitching staff that could really pitch. If the White Sox went into extra innings tied at 2-2, we would say that the White Sox were leading 2-2. Because if Billy Pierce or any of the starters pitched, and Hoyt Wilhem was releiving, it was over. Jim Rivera stole home once, and we couldn't get William Pritchett to stop talking about it. In those early years, my favorites were Minnie Minoso, Sherman Lollar, Billy Pierce, Sandy Consuegra, Juan Pizzarro, Hoyt Wilhelm, and Virgil Trucks.

Figure 10.
The Chicago Public School Military Academy Formerly "The Eighth Regiment"

My good friend " Frank Bacon died in 2003. He was a member of my college fraternity, an Army General, and Superintendent of the Chicago Public School Military Academy. His funeral took place here, and every newsworthy black personality was present, including more than 250 Kappas. His wife, Gloria Jackson-Bacon, an MD, founded the Altgeld Garden Health Clinic. It is so ironic because two years earlier, one of my closest friends in my life, Army General Ben Waller, who lived less than a block south of the Military Academy, passed away. Ben was a state champion in the half mile, and the mile relay team. I only learned from Dr. Don Smith in 2003, that Ben Waller was Adjutant to Commanding General Schwarzkopf, in the Desert Storm War, in Iraq. Ben was also editor of the Phillips Journal, the school newspaper, and a member of the Social Club " the Gentlemen". I was President, and Ben was the only reason that William Pritchett and I were on the newspaper. We were known as "Scoop" and "Flash", and I'm not sure in which order we were identified. Ben lived two doors away from Louis Satterfield, another club member, who played saxophone for " Earth, Wind, and Fire, Tina Turner, and Phil Collins. Louie lived between Quincy Jones, and Phillips High

School Graduate, and City of Chicago Police Superintendent, Terry Hillard, who retired in 2003, at a smashing event at the United Center, where the Chicago Bulls played basketball.

The Eighth Regiment Armory was the site of the introduction of the "Tucker Automobile". It was fabulous, and we couldn't wait until it could be seen driving down our streets. It never happened. The movie, "Tucker" that came out in the nineties, explained that the major manufacturers of automobiles didn't want the competition.

Eighth Regiment Armory

Address: 3533 S. Giles Ave.
Year Built: 1914-15
Architect: J.B. Dibelka

Date Designated a Chicago Landmark:. September 9, 1998

This was the first armory in the United States built for an African-American military regiment. The "Fighting 8th" traces its roots to the formation of the volunteer Hannibal Guard militia in 1871. It later became a division of the Illinois National Guard and during World War I was incorporated into the 370th U.S. Infantry (also see <u>Victory Monument).</u> After the armory closed in the early-1960s, it became the South Central Gymnasium. In1999, following an extensive renovation, it was reopened as a public high school. It is one of nine structures in the <u>Black</u> Metropolis-Bronzeville Historic District.

9. Copyright 2003 City of Chicago Department of Planning and Development, Landmarks Division

http://www.ci.chi.il.us/Landmarks/E/EighthRegiment.html

CLARKS POOLROOM

I was fourteen years old when William Pritchett, and I decided to start shooting pool. We were admitted without incident at Busters Pool Room on 39th Street, at Indiana Avenue. The law stated that you had to be "18" to participate. But at "Busters", obviously, no one cared. I decided to try entering Clarks Poolroom on 35th at Indiana. Tom Clark was all poised to throw me out when the poolshooters laughed, and told him to "let me stay". I stayed until I was a junior in college, and our family moved to

Memoirs of Bronzeville

Chatham. Every poolroom had a "shark", or a player who played for the house. Joe, who always referred to himself as "Po Joe", was the resident "shooter". He won consistently, until a man named "Walter" visited one afternoon. Walter was so good at his craft, that he was only allowed to shoot with one hand, and was known fondly as the "one armed bandit". The player could choose his game: "bank", "nine ball", "eight ball", or "one pocket". If the player chose "one pocket", he could save himself some time, sign his payroll check, and just give it to Walter. I never saw Walter walk out of a poolroom without winning money. At age 18, Walter hired me to hold his money, and place bets for him. I was very pleased, because I never had less than fifty dollars on me, from my cut. My family wondered where I was getting so much money, and quickly put an end to it. They felt that it was unlawful, and too dangerous.

I shot pool for free with the owner, Tom Clark, when business was slow. My regular partner was a 6'6" policeman named Smitty. One of my other special friends was a man named Scurlock. Scurlock had a long rap sheet with the police, which was not unusual in any of the poolrooms. He had once decided to take a vacation to California by robbing service stations along the way. He was a big bruiser, and was funny. I don't know why we were friends, but we simply "clicked". Scurlock also liked to tease other people, when he wasn't taking his fun out on me. There were professional boxers in the neighborhood, and the only way that they could survive was to be sponsored by a restaurant, and other characters, normally gamblers. Scurlock was teasing the boxers in the poolroom one day, and challenged them to an exchange of blows to the midsection, for $50.00. One of the boxers broke several of Spurlock's ribs, and it was known all over the neighborhood. Scurlock, of course was not the only joker in the poolroom. When one of our friends heard about the ridiculous bet, he approached Scurlock. " Hey, Scurlock". I heard you paid Jimmie $50.00 to crack your ribs, how much would you give me if I cut your throat?

The Black All Star game was held at Comiskey Park, and Tom Clark would close the pool room, and we would all go. This was when I received my history lesson in relation to black pro sports. The poolshooters knew all about Satchell Paige, Josh Gibson, and Cool Papa Bell, who was so fast that he could turn out the lights, and jump in the bed before it was dark in the room. The best liars and story tellers undoubtedly grew up in poolrooms across the country. I was always spellbound in their presence. They related to me that the white all- stars that I watched were not as good as the black players, and when the white teams barnstormed during the off season, they were beaten repeatedly by the black players. The local team was the "Chicago American Giants". Others were the "Pittsburg Crawfords", "Indianapolis Clowns", "Memphis Red Sox", the "Birmingham Black Barons", et al. I had the same sensation watching the baseball game that I had when I watched the all white basketball teams on television. I could walk outside in the neighborhood and see better basketball from Walter Hicks, from St. Elizabeth High School, Sweet Charlie Brown from Du Sable, and other players from Phillips, and Dunbar High Schools.

The first job that I received other than the U.S. Post Office was the result of one of my friends in the poolroom. I was told to report to a man named Saul Burkson of Burke Shade Company. Mr. Burkeson was marvelous. When I completed my college classes for the day, I went to work for six hours a day at his company. The regular workers worked from 8-4pm. Mr Burkeson hired two friends to keep me company, and allowed some of the regular day workers to work overtime, with me in charge. He also hired friends of mine from high school, when the Lawrin Lamp Company, the associated company, had a flood and needed short term workers for the summer. I also was allowed to drive Mr. Burkeson's new white Oldsmobile. I was in heaven, but when my grades arrived for the summer, my father had called Mr. Burkeson, and told him that I could no longer work in the summer, and I was to apply myself to studies until my grades improved. I was a Sophomore at the time, and I was not allowed to work again until my senior year, with the exception of Christmas at the U.S. Post Office during the winter school break.

CHAPTER TWO

**Figure 11.
Raymond School**

My father enrolled me in kindergarten at age four. When my class was passed on to the first grade, I was left behind, so technically, I flunked kindergarten. I was home with the mumps, measles, and chicken pocks, or as they were known in the neighborhood : chicken pops. I was later re-enrolled as a kindergartener, but when the teachers gave me books to read, it was very easy for me because I had read every basal reader from first through fourth grade at home with my siblings. The grades were different then, and children were passed to the next grade every semester, instead of every school year. I was passed from 1C to 1B to 1A in one week where I rejoined my kindergarten class, and remained with them throughout my elementary school education.

Before we had "Educable Mentally Handicapped" " Behavior Disordered", "Emotionally Disturbed", Trainable Mentally Handicapped, and "Moderate Learning Disabled", there was the "Dummy Room". They were all lumped into one room. My buddies and I determined that if we ever got the chance, we might get in there for a couple of weeks. They were on field trips every week to some of the most interesting places in Chicago, and we normally had to wait until May to start " field trips" with our class. We figured that they weren't so dumb after all.

We were in the fourth grade when Arthur Donohue's father arrived in the afternoon. We had just come in from lunch, and the teacher, who was an excellent teacher, explained to Arthur Donahue's father that she had to call him because Arthur was out of control. Arthur's father must have been about Six feet- four inches, but he seemed much taller to us. I want you to understand that these were the days before negotiations between parents and children. I don't think that there was a "Department of Children and Family Services", because they could have backed that truck up, and took away almost every adult female on my block. When the teacher had finished explaining to Arthur Donohue's father, he walked over and took his son outside the classroom door, took off his belt and gave Arthur a savage beating. Arthur reappeared crying, and standing. I don't think that he sat down that entire afternoon. The teacher then attempted to teach class. Not one student responded to anything that she said, because we were afraid that Arthur Donohue's father was coming back.

My next episode with Arthur Donohue came two or three years later, in the sixth or seventh grade. Unfortunately, some teachers had the unpleasant habit of placing a student in charge of the room, when they had to leave. The student was then responsible for telling the teacher, "who was talking". Arthur was, of course "talking", and I related the matter to the teacher. I knew that this meant that I had to fight. Fighting didn't really upset me. However, my mother had a crazy rule that her children should not get involved in a fight, no matter what. She also had a codicil that said, "don't ever get in trouble in school, upon pain of death". Classes were let out in rows of two's, and I was in the front. I quickly ran across the street to get off school property, and out of sight of the crossing guards. The entire class followed. I fought with Arthur until somebody broke it up. I then went to a friend's house to check for torn clothing, and evidence of a "fight". When I became a principal, one of my first rules was, "don't leave a child in charge of your classroom". We'll send up an aide, or someone to watch your class.

The next time I was left in charge of a classroom was in eighth grade and John Smith, who was to become a starting tackle, as a freshman, on the Phillips Wildcats High School football team, was talking. I reported it to the teacher, and waited outside for my beating. Fortunately, John liked me and told me to forget about it.

It was a serious matter for any mother to be spotted heading in the direction of the school. If she came in, the unlucky student was sure to hear about it in seconds. We used the same drill that always worked when mothers came home from work. We told them how happy we were to see them, and if we could be of any assistance. I don't think that we ever fooled any of them, but they always nodded politely, thanked us, and went to the office, then to the child's classroom. As long as that parent was in the building, everyone was on their best behavior, because if your mother got a bad report, that was just as bad as having been guilty of something.

I'm sure that I mentioned that the black women in my neighborhood laughed and joked, but they did not play. The toughest boy in my neighborhood had displeased his mother. We were playing softball when she appeared. For a mother to appear at an athletic event meant "trouble", and when she approached Baldy and delivered a vicious right hook knocking him to the ground. No one moved. She explained in "soft tones" why she was unhappy, turned and left. Every one of us wanted to laugh, but we knew that if we did, we would not survive the beating that he was sure to give us, either individually or collectively. I think I must have drawn blood biting my lip. We all looked sympathetic until Baldy followed his mother home. When he was way out of sight, we discussed what a wonderful right cross she had, and Baldy must have inherited her skills. Then we laughed.

TEACHER DEDICATION AT RAYMOND SCHOOL

I'm sure that everyone felt that their teachers were the best, perhaps because many remembered only the good things, while a minority only remembered "the bad". I remember teachers who taught me until I knew the subject, who took their lunch periods to stay with the class, and the two Physical Education teachers, who taught us to dance the formal social dances: i.e. the "waltz', and fox trot . We also went on constant field trips to the <u>Bowman Diary</u>, the Lincoln Park and the Brookfield Zoos, <u>The Chicago Public Library</u>, and all of the city museums. I received my first library card in the third grade, while on a field trip to the Chicago Public Library, in downtown Chicago.

**Figure 12.
The Bowman Diary**

The Bowman Diary, on 41st at Wabash, was the center of many field trips for Raymond School students. I remember milk and cookies given to each of us when we were seated, and shown a movie about "Milk, the perfect food". When I took this picture in 2003, the Bowman Diary had been closed for many years. The title had been painted over, and the space is now owned by another company.

**Figure 13.
The Southside Community Art Center**

I was enrolled in special art classes at the school, and the Art Center on 38th at Michigan. I could go downtown to the <u>Art Institute of Chicago</u>, for further free instruction, if I chose. I made childhood decisions, and chose to play with my friends on athletic teams instead. One teacher at Raymond School asked if I would accept a scholarship to the Wabash "Y" on 38th at Wabash. I had to explain that I could not come into this neighborhood alone after school. It was too dangerous.

Figure 14.
The Art Institute Of Chicago

Equal parts museum and academic institution, The Art Institute of Chicago has been a fixture on the creative landscape since its founding by a group of artists in 1866. With a famous pair of bronze lions standing sentry, the not-for-profit organization's museum houses some 320,000 works of art in a dozen collections ranging from Asian art to architecture to textiles. The institute's more than 2,200 students pursue certifications, undergraduate degrees, and graduate degrees in fields such as art, fashion design, painting, sculpture, and writing. The Art Institute of Chicago is also home to the Ryerson and Burnham Libraries, which together constitute one of the world's largest art museum libraries.

10. HTTP:// WWW.ARTIC.EDU

On Monday, October 11, 1897, the Central Library opened its doors to the public, and the 24-year dream of a permanent home for the Chicago Public Library was realized. The building, located on the grounds of Dearborn Park, (named for the Fort Dearborn Military Reservation that formally encompassed the area) at Michigan Avenue between Washington and Randolph Streets, cost approximately $2 million to design and build. The building was designed by A.H. Coolidge, associate of the firm Shepley, Rutan & Coolidge of Chicago. In designing this building, 25 draftsmen took one year to complete approximately 1,200 drawings. Heedful of the lessons of the Chicago Fire, they designed the building to be practically incombustible.

The Central Library combined the unique architectural concepts of the 1890s with the ideals of the American library movement of the period:

11. Copyright 2003 City of Chicago Department of Planning and Development, Landmarks Division

http://www/chipublib.org/003cpl/cpl125/central.html

Figure 15.
The Chicago Cultural Center
On Michigan Avenue Formerly,
The Chicago Public Library

The bill to erect and maintain a public library on the grounds of Dearborn Park also required the inclusion of a Soldiers' and Sailors'

Memorial Hall to "commemorate and forever bear witness to the patriotism and sacrifices of the Soldiers and Sailors from Illinois who took part. [in America's Civil War]." The collection was named for the Grand Army of The Republic Society and contains uniforms, rare documents, medical instruments and armaments. Today the G.A.R. collection is held in the <u>Special Collections Division</u> of the <u>Chicago Public Library</u> in the <u>Harold Washington Library Center.</u> Parts of the collection are displayed annually in the Grand Gallery and throughout the building.

In 1970, after over 70 years of continuous operation, with only minimal maintenance and repairs, the Central Library building began showing signs of age. Space was inadequate for the large book collection. The mechanical, electrical, communication and heating systems were obsolete and inadequate. In some quarters of the city it was suggested that the building be demolished and the Library moved elsewhere, turning the property over to commercial interests. These ideas were quickly put aside when the Library building was given historic architectural and landmark status in November of 1976.

In 1974, the Board of Directors authorized a massive renovation of the aging Central Library building, a process that took three years and cost $11 million. The architectural firm of Holabird & Root developed the renovation plan. When the Chicago Public Library Cultural Center opened in October of 1977, it was able to provide free access not only to books and other materials, but also a year-round schedule of free programs, lectures, films, plays, concerts and exhibits.

Although the total renovation of the old Central Library was a great success, there was still a need for more space for the Library's growing collections. Opinions varied between adding on to the existing building or constructing an entirely new building. After years of debate and discussion among the Library Board and the Chicago City Council, <u>Mayor Harold Washington</u> determined that the City should build an

entirely new building for the Central Library. Today, the former Chicago Public Library is known as the <u>Chicago Cultural Center</u> and is home to many arts programs as well as the offices of the City of Chicago's <u>Department of Cultural Affairs.</u>

Memoirs of Bronzeville

A NEW CENTRAL LIBRARY: THE HAROLD WASHINGTON LIBRARY CENTER, 1991

The designated site for the new Central Library was 400 S. State Street, a one and-one-half block tract in the South Loop area. On July 29, 1987, Mayor Washington and the City Council authorized a design/build competition and approved a bond issue to finance the project.

Under the rules of the competition, architects and builders teamed up to design the new Central Library within the set price of $144 million. The design/ build approach assured that the City's expense was limited to the cost of the bond issue. The design/build team was selected based on both design and cost criteria.

The design selection process as well as other building plans included significant input from citizens' groups, architectural experts and government officials.

On Monday, June 20, 1988, at 9:33 a.m. in the Library's Cultural Center auditorium, Norman Ross, Chairman of the Citizen Jury, announced to the Library Policy Review Committee that of the five entries, the vote was 9-2 in favor of the SEBUS group's proposal. The SEBUS Group included U.S. Equities, developers; Hammond, Beeby & Babka, Inc., design architects; Schal Associates, Inc., general contractors; A. Epstein and Sons, International, architects of record and structural engineer; and Delon Hampton & Associates, architects and engineers.

The Library Board decided that the new Central Library would be named after the late Mayor, Harold Washington, the city's first African American mayor, a great lover of books and advocate of the Chicago

11. The Chicago Public Library's Harold Washingon Library Center, 400 South State Street.

37

Robert Brazil

History of the Chicago Public library: Windows of Our Past
http://www.chipublib.org

The teachers were probably grossly underpaid during my early years, because services to students were quite extensive. We took showers through the third grade. I remember with horror, because we had a female attendant, and I raced for my towel, whenever her back was turned. We also had regular shots by the resident doctor, and dental check-ups by the resident dentist. Mrs. Douglas, the librarian made sure that I read a book every week, and I'm sure that she extended the same privilege to many other students, as well. I learned to sew in home mechanics, on machines that were electric, and some that had to be pumped by foot. I sewed aprons, and items that were useful in the kitchen. We don't have those classes anymore.

CHAPTER THREE

SOCIAL LIFE IN THE NEIGHBORHOOD AND CHICAGO

A favorite activity in the neighborhood was the abundance of "quarter parties", or "rent parties", if the host or hostess charged more. This was where you learned to dance, and got to know the relationships between boys and girls when they were not in school. I don't remember attending " quarter parties", after elementary school. Phillips High School had a social center on Friday nights, where you could roller skate in the girls gym, swim, participate in games, or dance. This replaced the quarter party activities for me.

- Somehow, we smaller kids had an opportunity to watch the "big boys", dance with girls. A younger sibling, a friend, allowed several of us pre-teens in to observe. I was surprised to see who the best dancers were. Several boys who had been considered "shy", actually had girls standing in line to dance with them. Several of the girls, dressed in a lot less clothes, that I was accustomed to seeing them in daily life.

- **JAZZ JOINTS IN CHICAGO: MODERN JAZZ ROOM, THE MODERN JAZZ QUARTET, LONDON HOUSE, OSCAR PETERSON BLUE NOTE, BRASS RAIL**

- My friends and I didn't wait until we were old enough to visit the jazz clubs in Chicago. We were now sixteen to eighteen years of age. We dressed in sport jackets, and ties, and had a regular Saturday night schedule for watching Miles Davis and John Coltrane, Dizzy Gillespie, and others at the jazz festivals, sometimes at the International Amphitheatre on 41st and Halsted. We occupied the $3.50 seats in the upper deck, until we were seated and moved to a better location. The Modern Jazz Quartet: John Lewis Milt Jackson, Percy Heath, Kenny Clarke and later Connie Kaye, played the Modern Jazz Room twice yearly. We never missed it. Oscar Peterson, and later, Ramsey Lewis held forth, at the London House. We frequently attended the Brass Rail, and the Blue Note, when our favorites were not in town. After a show, we would retire to the Pershing Lounge on 64th at Cottage Grove for Ahmad Jamal, and later, "Young John Young". Wes Montgomery and Brother Jack Mc Duff were our favorite organists. Other jazz favorites were: Art Tatum, Louie Armstrong, Ray Charles, Charlie Parker, Lionel Hampton, Errol Garner, Thelonious Monk, Count Basie, Duke Ellington, Lester Young, Frank Wess, Lou Donaldson, Billy Taylor, Clifford Brown, Max Roach, and Sonny Rollins.

- The management knew that we were underage, and policemen were present at all times. But, if we behaved ourselves, and drank non-alcoholic drinks, then we were welcome. Besides, it would have been very un-cool to act up in a jazz set.

- Our favorite singers were Dinah Washington, Nancy Wilson, Ella Fitzgerald, Etta James, Ruth Brown, Sarah Vaughn, Billie Holiday, Tina Turner, Billy Eckstein, Joe Williams, Peggy Lee, Dave Lambert, Jon Hendricks, and Annie Ross of Lambert, Hendricks, and Ross, Sammie Davis, Jr., and the great Nat "King"Cole.

- White Jazz musicians were not in short supply. We enjoyed Chet Baker, trumpet, Bob Brookmeyer on the valve trombone, Kai Winding of J and K fame, teaming with JJ Johnson on trombone, Terry Gibbs on the vibra harp, Gerry Mulligan, the baritone saxophone, Gene Krupa, drums, Paul Desmond, saxophone, and Herbie Mann, flute.

- You did not have to go downtown to enjoy a lively evening in Chicago. The hot spots were: Mc Kees Lounge, The 711 Club, The Pershing Lounge, Budland, Basin street, Muddy Waters on 35th Street, at Smitty's Corner on the northwest corner of Indiana Avenue. The Jazz Clubs were outstanding, and not too expensive. The Pershing Lounge, on 64th at Cottage Grove, and the Sutherland Hotel on 47th at Drexel, were the jazz centers that I frequented. I knew about the jazz clubs on 43th near Indiana, The Palm, and the Checkerboard Lounge, but they were not two of my stops.

- Salsa is currently back in style. When I attended high school and college, we did the mambo at Budland on 64th at Cottage Grove, on Tuesday nights, and Basin Street, on 63rd at Cottage Grove, on Fridays. I haven't seen better Latin dancers, even when I visited Rio De Janeiro, Acapulco, Mexico City, Buenos Aires, or Aruba. There was a mixture of hispanics, blacks, and some whites that were simply amazing to watch. There were contests and prizes to the best dancers.

Figure 16.
Russell Lee, April 1941. Negro Cabaret p. 89.
Stange, Maren [2003] <u>Bronzeville, Black Chicago in Pictures 1941-1943</u>. New York: The New Press.

I never got a chance to go to Club De Lisa, and the men in my neighborhood talked about it constantly. So, I was very jealous. It closed before I could attend. I did get a chance to watch the shows at the Grand Terrace on 35th at Calumet. Because it was hot, the doors were left open, and there was no air conditioning. I stood on the street, and watched a Cabaret Show that was equal to the Las Vegas shows for theatre and dancing. Later, when I visited Nevada, I realized that the Las Vegas costumes were much more expensive. The "open door policy" also allowed me to watch the blues performers, highlighted by the Muddy Waters Band, at Smitty's corner on 35th at Indiana.

Figure 17
This Is The Corner That Contained The Blues Bar "Smitty's Corner". Muddy Waters Played Here When He Came To Chicago. We Watched From The Street For Free.

CHAPTER FOUR

PHILLIPS HIGH SCHOOL

Figure 18
Wendell Phillips High School 2003

Some black parents complained in early 1916 that the instruction their children received compared unfavorably with what was available in white schools. Only Wendell Phillips High School, built in 1904, offered full facilities. Despite that school's symbolic importance to migrants, few had children with sufficient education to attend a Chicago high school immediately upon arrival.

Even Chicago's worst schools, however, could seem impressive to black newcomers from the South. Migrants from Georgia, where 85 percent of the schools attended by blacks operated in one-room buildings often without blackboards or desks, were unlikely to be disappointed when they walked into a Chicago school. Many southern counties did not provide funds for black schoolhouses; classes were taught either in whatever structures local blacks could afford to build or in buildings designed for other purposes. The oldest school in the South Side ghetto—Moseley Elementary School, built in 1856—had cooking facilities, manual training equipment, and a gymnasium. Even the school's unwieldy forty to one student-teacher ratio still seemed low by southern standards. In Jackson, Mississippi, classes in the two black schools ranged from 75 to 125 pupils. Atlanta's ratio of sixty-five to one, which resembled statistics for rural Alabama, was little better. Many migrants were accustomed to raising children with only minimal access to any school. In Georgia, Alabama, and Louisiana, less than half of all black children under ten years old attended school at all in 1910; in Mississippi the proportion reached 55 percent. Among children ten to fourteen years old, attendance was only slightly higher, ranging from 45 percent in Louisiana to 71 percent in Mississippi Those who did attend school had had little hope of receiving more than a basic education. Few black southerners living in states that sent large numbers of migrants to Chicago lived anywhere near a high school *they* could attend; in 1915, Mississippi, Alabama, Georgia, and Louisiana had a total of six public secondary schools open to black students, and only two of these offered a full four-year curriculum. Private institutions, funded by religious associations or northern philanthropy, provided only widely scattered options.

In Chicago, migrants could look forward to their children graduating from elementary schools and attending Wendell Phillips High School, with its impressive drill companies, laboratories, shops, domestic science rooms, gymnasiums, and other modern facilities.

Within the context of the experience of most migrants, therefore, Chicago's schools epitomized northern opportunity. State law prohibited segregation, and Chicago schools had been integrated formally since 1874. Although school officials took advantage of court rulings permitting them to gerrymander district lines, total racial segregation was impossible. Blacks were effectively excluded from most of the city's schools, but many of those into which they were "segregated" included a significant number of whites. As late as 1920, after four years of heavy migration had increased the concentration of Chicago's black population, every school attended by blacks had some white students. There were all-white schools in the city; but a migrant accustomed to Jim Crow schools could proudly write home that "I have children in school every day with the white children.

Many adult migrants, eager to educate themselves as well as their children, soon learned that working people also had access to good

schools. At Wendell Phillips Night School, adults could enroll in any elementary grade for the minimal fee of one dollar and in high school two dollars (the fees were refunded it the student attended at least three-fourths of the classes). Most migrants entered in the elementary grades. With the night school catering mainly to blacks even offered Afro-American history and literature by 1920—there was no question that blacks were welcome in these evening classes, taught by regular day faculty. Newcomers from the South flocked into the school, with enrollment increasing dramatically soon after the first wave of migration in late 1916. Teachers reported an "unusual" eagerness to learn, and the school quickly grew into the largest night school in Chicago. In 1921, nearly four thousand black Chicagoans were enrolled, with an average nightly attendance of two thousand. The evening school was one urban institution to which the migrants had little difficulty adjusting; it offered direct and unconditional access to an institution that they considered central to their full participation in American society.

Migrants needed even less encouragement to comply with the Illinois compulsory education law, a welcome contrast to southern policy. Many white southerners, especially in rural areas, still believed that blacks not only did not need education, but were ruined by schooling because it "unfits them for work." At some times during the especially cotton-picking season—planters wanted children in the fields and forced schools to close until the crops were in. Committed to an economy powered by an unskilled labor force, the South had little to gain from educating black children. What it had to lose were laborers who, if too well educated, might leave. Black southerners who wished to keep their children in school for nine months out of every year faced a task that was at best difficult and usually impossible.

By contrast, Chicago not only offered comparatively good schools, but encouraged children to attend regularly for the full school year. The city's political and business elite, along with its vocal reformers, agreed on the essential social role of the city's schools for working-class children. Basic education could provide the socialization necessary for ready adaptation to industrial work discipline, the skills appropriate to a dynamic manufacturing economy, and the ideological integration to cope with what the Tribune called "the dangers of citizenship lacking in intelligence and self-respect." This imperative to socialize a working class that would otherwise be inefficient as well as socially volatile combined with humanitarian sympathy for youthful toilers, to stimulate considerable pressure in favor of schooling over child labor. Although school authorities did not enforce the section of the state compulsory education statute which required unemployed sixteen- and seventeen-year-old children to attend school, they did take seriously their obligation to require and encourage younger children to attend school. While southern black children were expected to work in the fields, taking time off for school when work was slack, northern black children learned from their teachers that few jobs existed for children and that the jobs available to uneducated adults were insecure. "Your job today is to go to school," children read in the bookmarks distributed in Chicago schools. To migrants, the message was clear: their children would get the education they had sought in coming North."

17. Grossman, James R [1989]. <u>**Land of Hope, Chicago, Black Southerners, and the Great Migration,**</u> **Chicago: The University of Chicago Press, p. 249.**

The question that I have always had is " why were the night school classes closed and replaced with G.E.D classes". The G.E.D. classes did not have the same impact as receiving a regular high school diploma. My sister Vera, who later became a math consultant, and principal, for Chicago Public Schools, tutored adults from the night school. I also tutored those adults, and when she joined a Mrs. Brown as a volunteer for the Beatrice Caffrey Youth Service, I became a camp counselor at Camp Illini in Marseilles, Illinois, and later volunteered at the Better Boys Foundation, and Marrilac Community House, on the West side of Chicago. My mentor was Mrs. Alfreda Duster, daughter, of Ida B. Wells, the famous reformer. The Ida B. Wells Projects, in our neighborhood was named after Mrs. Duster's mother. Our parents would not allow us to accept money. The people kept trying to pay us, but we knew better than to accept anything. I always felt that this action by city officials was to keep the " disenfranchised" in their place. Many parents could go to work, cook the evening meal, and walk out of the door to go to " night school". The classes were transferred to the community colleges, where the adults would have to again get on a bus and travel some distance to the closest classes with a less rewarding diploma. This was not limited to black families. I later discovered that immigrants, at schools, such as Schurz High School, were later relegated to the same faith.

Carl Boyd, one my lifelong friends asked me to write the foreword to his book, The Last of the " Old School" Educators", highlighting Dr. Virginia Lewis. I happily complied, and demonstrated how I saw Dr. Lewis.

FOREWORD
LAST OF THE "OLD SCHOOL" EDUCATORS
DR. ROBERT BRAZIL   FORMER PRINCIPAL
CHICAGO SULLIVAN H.S.
ASSISTANT PROFESSOR UNIVERSITY OF ILLINOIS, RET.
DIRECTOR, THE PAIDEIA INSTITUTE OF HYDE PARK

Carl Boyd tries to define what our neighborhood was like with Wendell Phillips High School as its' center and Dr. Virginia Lewis as the Matriarch [Queen, Czarina.. etc.]

I entered Phillips High School as a 13 year old in 1953 where I was introduced to Ms. Lewis who was called by that name even, after she and her husband Bob, had received their Doctorate Degrees from Harvard. Dr. Lewis had this notion that once you were her student, you remained so for life with no back talk. There were many proofs of this and a few come to mind.

Dr. Henry Springs, the Track Coach and Assistant Principal, won many City and State Championships with several of "The World's Fastest Humans like Jim Golliday and Ira Murchinson. Dr. Springs was the speaker at Dr. Lewis' Retirement Dinner in Chicago and was relating to marching orders that Dr. Lewis was giving to all of us who were her charges. The place was packed and they all laughed because they thought that he was referring to High school days. After they calmed down, he explained that he was referring to last week. Dr. Springs was a Sub-District Superintendent at the time and Dr. Lewis was the Assistant Superintendent in Charge of Human Relations. for the Chicago Board of Education.

The Class of 1955 decided to hold an Alumni Weekend for ten classes or more. The Speaker for this occasion was, of course, Dr. Lewis. We were all laughing about all the success that we had after such a marvelous education at Phillips and the amazing faculty. We also were going to tell

Dr. Lewis that it was about time that she started treating us like adults, and not like high school freshmen.

She entered the room, we shuffled our feet, and you never heard so many

"yes ma' am"and -no ma'ams". She then rose to speak to us, and we all stood up from our seats at attention. She spoke to several hundred alumni for forty five minutes with no assistance from a microphone, and you could hear every word that she said.

When Carl Boyd called me and allowed me to watch the video of his interview with Dr. Lewis, I was enthralled. Carl's brother, David, was one of my high school buddies, and Carl attended Phillips Elementary School, where Dr. Lewis was principal, Carl later taught at the elementary school where I was principal. Carl was named " Outstanding Chicago Teacher" that year, and proved it was no fluke, when he repeated the process in Kansas City.

I received a birthday card from Dr. Lewis after I had mailed her a copy of my third book, <u>Beyond This Place, There be Dragons. The Chicago Public Schools Probation Process   www.first Books. com 1991.</u>

She called me to thank me and told me that she had heard that I was talking about her behind her back. I, of course, denied any transgressions on my part, and asked her, " What had she heard"?' I had to know which lie to defend. She then related to me the following: I had told close friends, particularly, Dr. Don Smith, my speech teacher and close friend [former President, The National Alliance of Black School Educators] that "The only reason that I kept going to school was to get that woman off my back." She told me that it was one of her proudest moments.

When I accepted my Bachelors Degree [not Cum Lawdy, but "Oh Lawdy"], Dr. Lewis called and let me know how proud she was and she knew that I was going to continue my education. I enrolled at De Paul University, and received my Masters Degree. The call came days later again informing me that her pride knew no limits, and she was preparing papers for me to enter a Doctorate Program and that she had some influence in accepting the "truly worthy?' I promptly applied for another exam that was given to prospective doctoral students nation-wide, and the local center was the University of Chicago. I was called by the University of Illinois, Champaign-Urbana, and was invited to take

Memoirs of Bronzeville

written, essay, and oral exams on campus. I was successful, enrolled and completed my studies in four years while working as the Principal of Parker High School, taking a one year sabbatical for residency, and finally was assigned to the position of Principal of Sullivan High School.

Dr. Lewis, I believe has some kind of computerized notebook, so that she can keep tabs on all of us, and I, for one, am forever in her debt.

12. Boyd, Carl [2001]. <u>Last of the " Old School" Educators</u> , Kansas City, Missouri: Advice

Media Publications 2001.

The faculty at Phillips was smart, and gave us all that they had to give. Mr. Henry Grant was the sponsor of our club, "The Gentlemen". I was the President. Maceo Thaddeus Bowie was sponsor of the Conservatives, and Dr. Donald Smith sponsored a club in his first year as a teacher at Phillips High School. We normally gave dances at the Grand Ballroom, but never without first hiring the school Policeman to man the door with us. The principal, Dr. Virginia Lewis also appeared with her husband, Dr. Robert Lewis. It was not unusual to have thirty or forty faculty members at any function that students gave.

I can only remember one incident where a student threatened a teacher. A young man transferred into Phillips and told displinarian Maceo Bowie,

[future president, Kennedy King College], what he could do with himself. A scuffle started, and we quickly grabbed the young man, and told him, " If he moved, it would be his last". Assistant Principal, Hank Springs grabbed Mr. Bowie, who yelled out in a high pitched voice, " Let me go Mr. Springs, I'll scratch his eyes out". We couldn't hold back the laughter, we released the young man, and told him to disappear.

A fellow student named Rose re-enrolled at Phillips, after a sabbatical from school. Rose transferred into my Senior Physics class and sat beside me. She asked me my name, and I lied, and told her that it was "Touchdown Brazil". Rose thought it was clever, and told me that she liked the way that I handled myself. I was a seventeen year old boy, and Rose was a twenty year old woman, and shake dancer. She was way out of my league, but I couldn't keep my big mouth shut. Rose showed up at my door, and my brother and father answered. When I saw who it was, and the look on their faces, I quickly turned Rose around, and walked her home. My father, and brother never seemed to stop teasing me.

Because we were teen age boys, we never stopped thinking of stupid things to do. Our latest mission was to take over for the cheerleaders at the next basketball game. Every nut in the school, and football player wanted in. We finally got our roster down to twenty, practiced as if our lives depended on it, and attended the next basketball game. The cheerleaders were led by Loretta Hall, who is still a good friend and chairperson of the Alumni Association. However, she is a "sistuh". I told the cheerleaders after one of their favorite cheers that "They couldn't cheer". They did what we knew they would do. They told us that if we didn't like the way that they cheered, to come down here, and do better, [expletives deleted]. With our mission accomplished, we filed out in order, lined up, rolled up our pants legs, and gave three perfect cheers. The crowd and the faculty went wild cheering us. However, Assistant Principal, Hank Springs wasted no time, in throwing us out of the game. The faculty allowed us back in within thirty seconds to watch the second half of the basketball game. I often wondered why my good friend, Hank Springs, waited until we had finished the third cheer before throwing us out. Based on his reputation, I didn't expect us to finish the first cheer.

Most of us learned to dance at home. My two older sisters, Lillian and Vera, were my first dance partners. I remember going to dances at college and watching girls dance together, because so many of the boys could not dance. There might have been one or two boys at Phillips who couldn't dance, but I didn't know them. I assumed that every boy could dance as well as the girls because dancers like David Boyd, Carl Boyd's brother, would put on a "show", and do a solo every now and then, because he thought that the girls couldn't keep up with his brilliance. We, of course, thought that we were the best dancers in the world. We came back down to earth when we visited Shell House, in the St. Elizabeth, and DuSable High School neighborhood. They were doing steps with a style that we had never seen. We watched, and then retreated to a safe place to practice.

Football was a big deal at Phillips. I saw my first Phillips-Dunbar football game, as a fifth grader, at the old Shrewbridge Field, or the dust bowl, as it was affectionately called. It was replaced, years later, by "Stagg Stadium", which had grass. The 1955 game between Phillips and Dunbar could not be held at a high school stadium. Dunbar had Willie Jones, a bruiser of a running back whose favorite play was the Southern California " Student Body Left or Right". I could swear that when they ran that play, which was often, they threw in two assistant coaches. John Scarbrough, the neighborhood quarterback was the Dunbar quarterback. I played, but not as much as John. We had Booker Benson, lineman and line backer, the best football player that I have ever seen, and Billy Martin at running back. Billy later played for the Army, the University of Minnesota, and the Chicago Bears. Billy was promoted from back-up to starter when Willie Gallimore, the Bear's star running back, was killed in an automobile accident. My brother told me that Booker Benson's brother, Theodore was better than he was. There were many other Bensons, all running backs, who were All- Public League football players.

My most embarrassing moment came in that same game. The score was 7-7, and Dunbar had to punt, late in the game, deep in their territory. I was to receive the punt, but my knee touched when I caught the ball. The game ended soon after. The poolroom, had of course emptied for the game, and my fellows were all in attendance. They were sympathetic, and patted me on the back to cheer me up. However, in church, at St. Luke Baptist Church, my miscue was revisited. As we kneeled in prayer, one of the adult females looked over at me, and asked, "Bobby, what did you drop that ball for?" I explained, while still kneeling that I didn't drop the ball, my knee touched the ground. The only other time that I got to field a punt was the next year against Tilden Tech, which was then an all-boys school, and very tough. The ball was punted over my head, I fielded it cleanly, and was headed back upfield when the referee ruled that I had stepped "out of bounds". I was five yards inside the field. An earlier call by one of the referees cost us a touchdown, when a Tilden Tech player ran far out of bounds, and we didn't tackle him because of an anticipated penalty. The player stepped back in and ran into the end zone. The referees never threw a flag.

I wrote for the school newspaper, "The Phillips Journal". I was the head sports writer when Phillips won the Illinois Tech Basketball Tournament in 1956. The games were played at the International Amphitheatre on 41st at Halsted. It was an historic time because I was graduating in January, and this was to be my last assignment. Ron Rubenstein, and another player named Dennenburg, were pure shooters and were the last of the "white super teams". They played an excellent game, and only lost to the powerhouse from Phillips 49-47. Rubenstein later became a national racquetball champion. Phillips won its' next two games, then defeated arch rival, Dunbar High School , followed by a close victory over Crane Technical High School, an emerging power on Chicago's west side, for the Illinois Tech Tournament Championship. Every Chicago Public School played in the tournament, and Phillips was favored to go on to win the city championship. However, Phillips lost their playoff game at Crane High school, later that year. There were ten games scheduled every day at the tournament, until the field was narrowed, later in the week. We all took lunches, and watched every game, and every seat was filled. Many Chicago teams were weakened because of January graduations in Chicago. The 1954 Du Sable High School basketball team with Sweet Charlie Brown, and Paxton Lumpkin, was probably the best high school team that Chicago has produced. They lost some of their best players to a January graduation, and Chicago eliminated January graduations years later. The Du Sable team lost to a downstate team, Mt. Vernon, in one of the most ill refereed games that I have ever seen. It appeared that any movement by a Du Sable player invited a traveling call by the downstate referees. Mount Vernon's best player, Al Avant, who was black, is presently the Athletic Director at Chicago State University.

" Every year, we were asked, "what kind of team do you have at Phillips this year?" Our response was always the same. "We have a tall dark team"."

I was accustomed to having Phillips win the city championship in track, because they had won for more than twenty consecutive years, when I entered the school. John Lattimore, Billy Martin, Ned Lenoir, Ben Waller, and many others were state champions in the dashes, long jumps, and relay teams. I believe that our team won the Illinois State Championship once or twice, during my time at Phillips. We could only practice field events at the University of Chicago Fieldhouse, which was rarely available. We had to win in the running events, because there was no place to practice, or improve in the pole vault, and some other related areas. My dream, as a principal, was always to have a field house built on the north, west, and south sides of Chicago, to give the Chicago Public Schools a more even playing field. It has never happened.

I'm not proud of my deviousness while attending high school. But it would be unfair for you assume that I was an angel. Whenever, a new teacher transferred into the school, we immediately had our connections in the print shop to produce paper passes to give our club members free access throughout the school. When principal, Dr. Virginia Lewis, ordered a locker clean-out, which happened several times a year, we had to empty our "pass locker", and each of us had to hold "passes" until homeroom was over.

There was an attic above the locker room at the Phillips gymnasium, that I only discovered, late in my tenure at the school. Before the locker room and gymnasiums were cleared out before a basketball game. We hid in the attic, and appeared later, while the game was in progress. I only did this once, because the attic was too crowded.

The only other anti-social exercise that I pulled off was the brilliant idea of taping the used basketball tickets back together. I noticed that they were only torn into two pieces, when they were collected at the door to the game. I collected the used tickets, applied scotch tape to the back, sold them for a quarter, and never attempted a rerun.

CHAPTER FIVE

MATRICULATION TO A HIGHER EDUCATION AND INTEGRATION

When I entered Chicago Teachers College in January, 1957, it was to be my most trying college experience. I was not very interesting, and I was a uninterested student. However, this was the beginning of large numbers of black students entering the school. We had to take a week of qualifying exams to enroll. Some students were allowed to enter, but they had to take non-credit courses, presumably to get them up to a college level of academic credibility. I never had any trouble with exams, and I had a disciplined high school experience, so I had little trouble taking the classes that I wanted. I graduated in three years, not because I was brilliant, but because I was desperate to start earning money.

I took a Sociology class, and was given an assignment to write a paper about the Black Muslims. Malcolm X was just beginning to get a national reputation.

He was speaking at a church located on the northeast corner of 54th at Greenwood, in Hyde Park. I attended several meetings, gathered what little research there was on the Black Muslims, and wrote a paper that exemplified the positives that the Muslims had engendered. They had gotten blacks to stop taking controlled substances, fed the poor, reformed criminals, and with the exception of calling white people "white devils, they weren't bad at all. When I turned in my paper, I was summoned to Dean Cook's office, and asked to explain myself to the Sociology professor, and other interested faculty. I explained that I was given the assignment by the professor. He never explained that he wanted me to write a report that was negative. If he had, I probably would have written on something else. I was dismissed, and I was never asked to write a controversial paper again, by any faculty.

I loaded up on classes, simply to graduate, by taking eighteen hours each semester, and taking eight hours each summer. When I graduated, the faculty stood up and applauded so long that I was unsure whether they were proud of me, or they were just happy to get me out of there.

I was never one to give much credence to grades. I knew that some students got better grades because they played up to the professor, and others because the professor simply liked them. I remember three circumstances that made me think differently about grades. I took a Kinesiology class because it represented four hours of credit, and would enable to get out of college faster. There were seven exams given. My average was 97. The next highest average was 83. Many class averages were in the 50's, and those students received C's. When I was given a "C", and the next highest grade below mine, received an "A", I went to the department head and had the situation corrected.

At DePaul University, I was not allowed to enter the Masters Program until December. De Paul, like most Chicago Colleges, had their most difficult, or "flunk out" classes, during the first quarter, or semester. I was probably lucky to miss that first quarter. By this time, I had stopped playing around, and was a serious student. I remember a statistics class that opened with fifty students. After the mid-term, there were twenty five of us. A Dr. Rezler, was German and serious. She was, however, a tremendous teacher of math. I was told that she had given only one

" A", in five years at De Paul. She, however, presented me with an "A". I surprised her by going to her office, hugging her with a kiss on the cheek. By the time, she recovered, I had already left her office. I also took an "Advanced Educational Psychology" class. The professor read directly from his notes. I memorized them, received a '100' on the midterm, and a "100" on the final. He awarded me a "C" for my efforts. I promptly went to the Dean of the Graduate School, Father Courtelou, whose brother was President of De Paul, and Dean Courtelou counseled me for the remainder of my two years at De Paul University.

DePaul University is the largest Catholic university in the US, with more than 20,000 students attending classes at its eight Chicago-area campuses. The school offers some 130 degree programs through its eight undergraduate and nine graduate colleges and schools. DePaul is also home to the well-regarded Kellstadt Graduate School of Business. Among DePaul's notable alumni are Chicago mayor Richard M. Daley, McDonald's chairman and CEO Jack Greenberg, and actor Gillian Anderson (*The X-Files*). DePaul was founded as St. Vincent College in 1898 by Vincentian Fathers.

13. http://www.depaul.edu.

At the University of Illinois, I received tremendous support from the faculty. However, a graduate student received my fee-waiver, and sent it back. When he was confronted, he said," I didn't deserve it". The only other incident came during the week long exam for doctoral students. My exam was not there, and I had to walk over to the College of Education to take the first day's exam away from the other students. The faculty at the University of Illinois handled everything in a very professional manner.

Figure 19.
University Of Illinois
The University Of Illinois Champaign-urbana

Illinois is a world leader in research, teaching, and public engagement, distinguished by the breath of its' programs, broad academic excellence, and internationally renowned faculty. Illinois alumni have earned Nobel and Pulitzer Prizes and Olympic medals, have orbited the earth and lead international corporations. The campus offers rich experiences beyond the classroom, from the best performing arts to Big ten sports.

Illinois has tremendous breadth and depth in academics, with more than 150 undergraduate and more than 100 graduate and professional programs. A preeminent faculty propels many academic programs to be ranked among the best in the world. This emphasis on vampus wide academic excellence has built Illinois' reputation as one of the nation's premier universities.

The original land grant mission of the University of Illinois farmers and industrial workers, create new knowledge through research, and share that knowledge with the people of the state.

Those core missions continue to guide the campus, but its' audience now spans the globe. Today, Illinois prepares students of various backgrounds to lead in an increasingly globalized world. Its' research examines the world's interrelated, critical issues, and its' public engagement activities touch every part of the earth.

14. www.uiuc.edu/

I was selected by Mrs. Martha Cleveland, who was Irish-American, to be her Assistant Principal at Tesla Elementary School. I made every mistake that you could make during my first year. She stuck with me and I am forever grateful. I improved rapidly after that first year. One day, She asked me why black people were so violent? I didn't take offense. I explained that blacks in this country have had to endure centuries of slavery, and have yet to attain a level playing field in our society. I thought that we were about to have a philosophical conversation, but, when I asked her about the Irish Republican Army, and war with the Protestants in Ireland, she became infuriated, and left the room. I didn't understand because blacks didn't get that excited about religious differences. When blacks were allowed to live mostly anyplace in Chicago, they usually moved from a Baptist neighborhood, and close to a Methodist, Presbyterian, Lutheran, or Episcopalian Church. They seemed to join without much fanfare. It was also common for black families to send their children to Catholic schools, because they believed that their children could receive a better education than the education which was offered in most Chicago Public Schools. My own family moved to Chatham to a house around the corner from Crerar Presbyterian Church, and my parents became members, until their deaths.

I was at my first general conference, and dinner of the Chicago Principals Association. The Chicago Board had just allowed a larger number of blacks to pass the Principals Examination, and I passed the 1970 exam. Three thousand educators, all with Masters Degrees, took the exam, and I believe that one hundred and ten had passed the written and oral parts of the exam. I'm not perfectly sure of the exact number. Also, this was the first time that communities were allowed to orally examine candidates for the principalship of their schools. I was sitting with my friends, a group of black principals, who had been chosen first, and we were receiving special instruction before entering the schools. We called ourselves The PhD.'s, or Phenomenal Darkies.

An officer from the head table called me up and asked me why all of the blacks were sitting together at two tables. I probably could have answered better, but this was too good to pass up. I responded that all of the other tables had all white people, and perhaps they might want to join us. The officer turned red. I knew what she wanted. She felt that it would have been better if we had broken up, and each of us would sit at a table with all white principals for a more positive Kodak moment. This is not an indictment of Chicago Principals. I found, in my career, that they proved not to give a damn about race, and my friendships with other principals were always positive, regardless of race. If you attended a principals conference today in Chicago, you would see the natural integration that the officer was looking for.

I recall a conversation with a close friend and fellow Phillips graduate, Dr. Robert Saddler, who was a Deputy Superintendent for Chicago Public Schools . I was relating how I was reading a book on the "culturally deprived", while a student at Northwestern University. I realized, after some study, that the writer was talking about us. I was at Northwestern for a summer institute. We had absorbed our culture, but realized that in order to be successful in our society, we had to truly learn   standard English, and relate to a culture that was foreign to us.

The Institute Grant occurred in 1965. I had received a summer fellowship to Northwestern University. There was a mixture of seasoned veterans from Chicago, and Detroit. The mix included regular graduate students from Northwestern University. The course was for eight hours of graduate credit, with a fee waiver, and stipend, allocated to each participant. Warner Saunders, from Television Station NBC in Chicago appeared one night to recruit tutors for the Better Boys Foundation at 1215 South Pulaski on Chicago's Westside. I tutored a third grade boy, and a fourth grade girl on Wednesday evening. They were never tardy or absent. I would stop by a Chandlers Bookstore in Evanston, and select small inexpensive gifts for my tutees. One night, the manager of the store asked me why I was selecting   childrens' gifts each Wednesday night. When I told him what I was doing. He told me not to pay for anymore gifts, and wished me good luck. I have always felt that when you are doing something positive, something good always seems to find its' way to you.

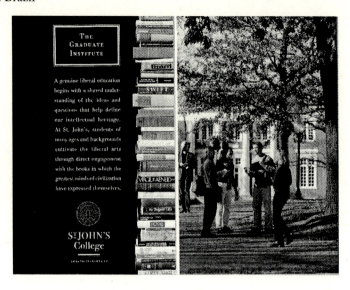

Figure 20.
St. John's College, Santa Fe, New Mexico www.sjcsf.edu/

In 1984, Mortimer J. Adler, invited Dr. Ruth B. Love, Superintendent of Chicago's Public Schools, to join his Paideia Group. They chose four schools to send faculty to St. John's College. Sullivan High School, Austin High School, Kilmer Elementary School which was across the street from Sullivan, and Goldblatt Elementary School, were chosen. The goal was to introduce instruction to students by Socratic questioning, coaching, and the didactic method, or lecture. We were sent to St. John's College for eight weeks of summer instruction, and and if we survived, four summers of graduate study, where we were to receive Masters Degrees from St. John's in the Arts and Sciences. Seventeen educators received Masters Degrees. This program launched the Paideia Institute of Hyde Park, an enrichment program for educators, which grew into a Masters, and Doctoral Program at the University of Illinois, Champaign-Urbana. It was reported to me that thirty seven educators from Chicago received their doctorate degrees. After taking graduate hours with me in Champaign, and at the University of Illinois- Chicago Campus, they would then join the Cohort of Dr. Fred Rodgers to continue and complete their studies. After several years of work in this area as the Principal of Sullivan High School, Assistant Professor at the University of Illinois, and Director of the Paideia Institute of Hyde Park, Dr. Adler named me, an Associate of the Institute for Philosophical Research. Dr. Adler wrote three books on the Paideia Proposal. I followed with <u>The Engineering of the Paideia Proposal</u>, <u>A Covenant for Change</u>, and <u>Beyond This Place, There Be Dragons: The Chicago Public School Probation Process.</u> All of this activity was followed by an invitation in 1995, to have Paideia Institute Graduates attend Exeter College, The University of Oxford, In Oxford, England. The Paideia Institute continues to have Fall Retreats at Interlaken Resort, Lake Geneva, Wisconsin.

Figure 21.
Interlaken Resort, Lake Geneva, Wisconsin

I was a school principal for more than twenty years, with some success. Other educators have asked me about my administrative style. I thought about the administrators who had been my early role models, and they were all female. Mrs. Malone was my assistant principal at Raymond School. Virginia Lewis was my secondary school principal. Patricia Weisberg was my principal for student teaching, and the principal at my first assignment as a teacher at Ruggles Elementary School. Martha Cleveland was my principal when I was assigned to Tesla Elementary School, as an assistant principal, and Margaret Krawczyk was my first sub-district superintendent, when I was assigned to Parkside Elementary School, as principal. Dr. Nina Jones served as a continuous mentor for me, in her assignment as Assistant Superintendent of Chicago public Schools. My first experience reporting to men in my professional career, occurred when Parkside school was transferred into a district, administered by Dr. Donald Blyth, in Hyde Park-Woodlawn. Later that year, I was assigned to a summer Head Start program, directed by future Deputy Superintendent of Schools, Dr. James G. Moffat.

I sometimes selected faculty that probably would have driven other principals "insane". However, to their credit, they piled up a large number of "Outstanding Teacher Awards". They would post signs in the school directed at me, i.e. " You may be better than us individually, but not collectively". They also passed out lapel pins to faculty with the message " Say No to RDB". They did this because I was always demanding "More". The Lunchroom and janitorial staff countered with lapel pins that read " Say Yes to RDB". The faculty also had requests for the lapel pins, from central office staff, because I was a "shameless beggar", for central office funds. The meanest trick that the faculty introduced, occurred during my semi-annual speech to "Give More to Students and Community". After I finished my most heartwarming, tear driven request, to "give me their all", they held up numbered cards, in the way that Olympic skaters are rated, and gave me mostly eights and nines.

CHAPTER SIX

HISTORICAL BACKGOUND

Dr. James Grossman, an Assistant Professor of history at the University of Chicago wrote a book in 1989, which Captivated me and an audience of 200-300 Chicago educators. The teachers were encouraged to purchase this book, as a foundation for educating Chicago's public school students.

Black southerners arriving in Chicago, generally knew where to go once they walked out of the train station. Like their counterparts in New York, who asked in Pennsylvania Station how to get to Harlem, most black migrants to Chicago upon alighting at the Illinois Central terminal requested directions to the South Side or

to State Street. People whose friends, relatives, or townspeople had preceded them sought out specific addresses; those who had no idea where to go were likely to be directed to the South Side. Whites would assume that all blacks "belonged" in the ghetto; blacks would reason that bewildered newcomers might obtain assistance from black institutions while avoiding the danger of straying into hostile white neighborhoods. The logic of such advice suggests the significance—if not the visibility—of Chicago's color line, as well as the importance of various aspects of community within black Chicago. Shaped by both the circumscribing influences of the white city that surrounded it and the demands of the migrants and "Old Settlers" who inhabited it, the emerging "Black Metropolis" on the South Side was divided along lines of class, region, and even age. But it remained a community nevertheless, unified by the implications of racial taxonomies.

In 1910, 78 percent of black Chicagoans lived on the South Side in a narrow strip of land known to whites as the Black Belt. Beginning at the edge of an industrial and warehouse district just south of the Loop (Chicago's central business district), black Chicago stretched southward along State Street for more than thirty blocks, remaining only a few blocks wide except at its northern end. The 1910 census counted 34,335 black residents in this growing ghetto, which was expanding slowly along its southern and eastern boundaries. Another 3,379 black Chicagoans lived on the West Side, while most of the remaining 6,389 lived in smaller enclaves in Englewood, the Near North Side, and scattered other districts. Only 1,427 lived on the city's North Side. Because of the lingering presence of some whites in black neighborhoods, especially those on the edge of the Black Belt and the smaller enclaves, many black Chicagoans lived in what might loosely be called an integrated setting; but with black people virtually restricted to certain areas of the city, the housing market was actually segregated.

This residential pattern had evolved during the previous quarter century, when Chicago's black population had increased from 6,480 in 1880 to 44,103 in 1910. As late as 1898, only slightly more than one-fourth of Chicago's black residents lived in precincts in which blacks constituted a majority of the population; more than 30 per-cent inhabited precincts at least 95 percent white. Yet black enclaves were already emerging, mainly on the South and near West Sides. Ward statistics understate this concentration of the black population, as blacks often occupied only a small sector in each ward. This consolidating trend accelerated along with black migration. Few white neighborhoods had ever accepted with equanimity the purchase of property by even a "respectable" black family, even before migration reached a level that might have remotely threatened whites with the specter of "invasion." As the black population began to increase, whites became still less likely to tolerate a black neighbor and more actively began to resist black settlement in their neighborhoods.

At the same time, black institutional development contributed to the growing vitality and self-consciousness of the emerging black neighborhoods, making them attractive to blacks who preferred avoiding white people and their prejudices. What one historian of Detroit's black community has called the "push of discrimination" and "the pull of ethnocentrism" combined to impel black newcomers toward the ghetto. Exclusion aside, many migrants sought their first homes in areas populated by other blacks, where they could be more comfortable and find familiar institutions. This dynamic of choice and constraint, heavily influenced by economic factors, resembled the experience of European immigrants to Chicago during this period, but the differences were significant. Unfamiliarity with English made the ethnic neighborhood essential for many Europeans; blacks had no comparable imperative. White immigrants tended to live near workplaces; blacks dispersed in service occupations, could not, and when they did obtain industrial employment they were excluded from neighborhoods adjoining

Chicago's major industries. European newcomers lived near others of their nationality but usually in an ethnically diverse neighborhood that could hardly be described as a ghetto. Whether middle or working class, black Chicagoans were less likely than members of other ethnic groups to share public space across ethnic but within class boundaries. More than any other group, black Chicagoans occupied neighborhoods defined by permanent characteristics. Neither cultural assimilation nor economic mobility promised significantly wider choices. The color line separated more than residences. State legislation prohibiting racial discrimination in schools, municipal services, and public accommodations was seldom enforced, and except on the streets and in the streetcars, blacks and whites seldom mingled. Black children attended schools with whites, but only because by 1915 the emerging ghetto was still neither compact nor homogeneous enough to enable the Board of Education to draw district lines that would go beyond merely assuring that as few schools as possible would have black students. Municipal institutions often segregated black clients or discriminated in the provision of services. Most voluntary associations and private institutions simply excluded blacks, thrusting on the community the dilemma of accepting segregation or doing without such institutions as the YMCA. On the whole, in 1915 black Chicagoans lived among black neighbors, sent their children to pre-dominantly black schools, and were excluded from most establishments catering to whites.

Blacks occupied a similarly limited place in Chicago's booming economy. Fewer than one black male in twenty—and virtually no black females— worked in an occupation that might be described as managerial, professional, or proprietary; even many of these operated marginal businesses. Most workers were unskilled, and few worked in industry. If Chicago was the "City of the Big Shoulders," with an economic base of heavy industry, construction, and transportation, black workers found themselves relegated to marginal roles. White immigrants from southern and eastern Europe had to accept the worst jobs in the city's industries, but blacks lacked access even to those positions. Sharing the racial attitudes of other Americans, industrialists in Chicago and other northern cities saw no reason to hire blacks when they had thousands of white immigrants to fill their factories. Blacks were considered to be useful as strikebreakers on occasion, but were generally discharged once the strike ended. Industrial managers drew upon a series of commonly held assumptions about work habits and aptitudes of various "races," and if most Eastern European groups suffered from images that kept them in unskilled positions, at least they were white. Where foremen controlled access to industrial jobs, black workers lacked access to the networks of community and kin that were central to recruitment patterns. Chicago and other northern cities offered mainly service jobs to blacks, and between 1900 and 1910 the number of black servants in Chicago increased by six thousand, nearly half the city's increase in black population during that period. Men were likely to work as porters, waiters, servants, janitors, or elevator operators; two-thirds of all employed black women in 1910 were either servants or hand laundresses, with most of the others performing some other type of service!

Despite this apparent homogeneity, however, black

Chicago—like other urban black communities—was divided along class lines. Severely truncated at the top, this class structure rested less on wealth or contemporary white definitions of occupational status (except at the highest levels) than on notions of "refinement" and "respectability" maintained by the upper and middle classes. The few professionals, some with professional connections to the white community, tended to dominate the highest rungs of the ladders, with businessmen close behind. Postal workers, Pullman porters, and servants employed by Chicago's wealthiest white families and best hotels constituted much of the solid middle class, which at its margins could also include other workers with stable incomes and some education. Stable income was at least as important as accumulated wealth, an uncommon phenomenon in the black community. "Respectability" frequently depended upon property ownership, membership in the appropriate organizations, and leisure habits. Church, club, or lodge activities conferred as well as signified status; symbols of respectability could include affiliation with one of the larger Baptist or African Methodist Episcopal Churches, a YMCA membership, or a Masonic identification card. Upper-class blacks, who considered themselves "refined" rather than merely "respectable", joined Episcopalian, Presbyterian, or Congregationalist churches, entertained according to specific rules of etiquette, and socialized only within a limited circle of acquaintances.

Until the late nineteenth century, this upper class—largely businessmen with white clientele and professionals who had won the respect of their white colleagues—dominated black Chicago's leadership and resisted attempts to organize alternative institutions catering to blacks. To do so, they argued, would imply their acceptance of segregation. This elite not only opposed racial segregation in principle, but also feared its likely impact on their own social lives and institutional relationships. Disdaining association with blacks who lacked their refinement, members of this thin upper stratum recognized that segregation would force their social life inward toward the black community, rather than outward as they hoped.`

Between 1900 and 1915 a new leadership emerged in black Chicago,

one with an economic and political base in the black community. The emergence of the physical ghetto coincided with widening racial discrimination in Chicago and other northern cities, which forced blacks to make decisions circumscribed by their exclusion from a variety of social and economic institutions. Increasing separation opened new opportunities for business, professional, religious, and political leadership, and by the first decade of the twentieth century, a new middle class had begun to replace an older elite unwilling to sacrifice integrationist principles and therefore wary of separate black institutions and a ghetto economy.

This new generation of black editors, politicians, business people, and ministers would dominate Chicago's black institutions during the Great Migration and construct the foundation of what by the 1920s would be known as a Black Metropolis. The southern origins of these prominent figures perhaps contributed to their continuing influence on newcomers. Robert Abbott, raised outside Savannah, Georgia, visited Chicago in 1893 as a member of the Hampton (Institute) Quartet performing at the Columbian Exposition. He returned four years later and in 1905 founded the Chicago *Defender*. *Louis* B. Anderson, born in Petersburg, Virginia, was also drawn to Chicago by the fair; by 1919, he was not only an alderman, but also Mayor William Hale Thompson's floor leader in the City Council. Born in Alabama, Oscar DePriest traveled to Chicago from Kansas in 1889 and worked his way up from a house painter to election as Chicago's first black alder-man in 1915. Thirteen years later he would climb even higher, as the first black congressman elected from a northern district. Reverend Archibald J. Carey, like DePriest the child of ex-slaves, came from Georgia in 1898 to serve as pastor of Quinn Chapel, the city's largest African Methodist Episcopal Church. Such notables, provided an image—and a self-image—of a prewar generation of migrants who built institutions, shaped a newly self-conscious black community, and dominated Chicago's growing black middle class".

Adapting Booker T. Washington's doctrines of racial solidarity and self-help to the northern city, these business leaders and politicians de-emphasized the fight for integration and dealt with discrimination by creating black institutions. Between 1890 and 1915 they established a bank, a hospital, a YMCA, an infantry regiment, effective political organizations, lodges, clubs, professional baseball teams, social service institutions, newspapers, and a variety of small businesses. The growth of the black community promised to multiply growing political influence and economic activity. Like Abbott, whose newspaper was partly responsible for the popularity of Chicago as a destination for black southerners, Chicago's black politicians and entrepreneurs saw the migrants as a source of votes and customers."Growth, however, also implied diversity, and neither the "old" nor "new" leadership in black Chicago was prone to tolerate those who did not measure up to their standards. The *Conservator*, Chicago's first black newspaper and the voice of prominent leaders in the late nineteenth century, frequently criticized "the seamy side" of black Chicago during the 1870s and 1880s. The Chicago Defender picked up the mantle in the twentieth century, with complaints about newcomers, and degeneration even before the Great Migration. Both newspapers couched these criticisms within the context of appeals for improvement, providing lessons for proper behavior while chiding lower-class blacks for giving the race a bad image.'2."- George Cleveland Hall, a prominent physician and personal friend of Booker T. Washington, typified the attitudes of many of his contemporaries. He served in official capacities in the NAACP as well as the Washingtonian National Negro Business League and later became one of the founders of the Chicago Urban League. In 1904, Hall voiced the attitudes of middle-class black Chicago concerning the need—and yet the impossibility—of maintaining the distance between classes in the black community:

Most black Chicagoans before the Great Migration, however, neither possessed Ilall's "cultivation and refinement" nor lived "shift-less, dissolute and immoral" lives. Laboring long days in menial occupations, they returned home tired. Women, especially, spent most of their waking hours working, as they had to combine traditional household chores with other employment. Nearly half of all black women in Chicago in 1910 worked outside the home (compared with slightly more than one-fourth of white women), and among poor families the proportion was even higher. Most of these people had migrated from the South and had found that whatever skills or hopes they carried with them, service occupations provided the only possibility of employment in Chicago. Their leisure activities offered respite from their backbreaking, low-status jobs. Enthusiastic worship and lively nightlife attracted the scorn of much of the middle class, but such activities already were central elements of what St. Clair Drake and Horace Cayton would later call "the world of the lower class" in black Chicago. By 1904 (if not earlier), the storefront churches later to be associated with the Great Migration had already begun to appear along State Street. Less spiritually inclined workers found release in petty gambling, the fellowship of the numerous saloons along the State Street "Stroll," or boisterous parties. By 1914, the rent party (later made famous in Harlem) had been improvised to leaven the struggle for subsistence with sociability and relaxation.

16._Grossman, James R [1989]. Land of Hope Chicago, Black Southerners, and the Great Migration. "Home People and Old Settlers". Chicago: University of Chicago Press. PP. 123-130

Figure 22
The Chicago Daily Defender 2003

This former Jewish synagogue was home to the *Chicago Defender* from 1920 until 1960. Founded by Robert S. Abbott in 1905, the newspaper became nationally known for its outspoken editorial policies on behalf of civil rights issues. The "Great Migration" of the early-20th century was largely initiated by *Defender* editorials urging African-Americans to leave the poverty of the South for new opportunities in the North. It is one of nine structures in the <u>Black Metropolis-Bronzeville Historic District.</u>

15. Copy right 2003 City of Chicago Department of Planning and development, Landmarks Division.

http://www.ci.chi.il.us/Landmarks/D/Defender.html

Those of the race who are desirous of improving their general condition are prevented to a great extent by being compelled to live with those of their color who are shiftless, dissolute and immoral. . . . Prejudice of landlords and agents render it almost impossible for [the Negro] to take up his residence in a more select quarter of the city . . . no matter . . . how much cultivation and refinement he may possess."

A friend disclosed to me a phenomenon that I had not envisioned. The projects at Stateway Gardens, and Cabrini Green were in the process of being replaced by expensive townhomes for middle class, integrated communities. A surburban white family, that had not moved, but remained when many black families moved from Chicago, was warned by their black neighbors to move. The blacks reported that "The kind of people who are going to be placed in Section 8 housing, in their neighborhood, were not the kind that they wanted as neighbors". The blacks sold their homes, and the white families soon followed.

Lawrence Otis Graham introduced a book in 1999, that I encouraged

educators, who attended our fall weekends at Interlaken, Wisconsin to purchase for background on how to approach the introduction of Black history in Chicago.

For years, members of the black elite in Chicago and elsewhere heard accounts of police brutality against innocent blacks in the inn city, but we too often reacted in the way that some white people reacted "That's too bad about *those* people," we would say. We felt detached and uninvolved because "those" people were another group—another class. "Poor blacks are not like us," we wrongly told ourselves. "They dont relate to us and we don't relate to them." In fact, some upper class blacks even expressed some cynicism, convincing themselves that perhaps the urban blacks had done something to justify brutal police treatment.

In retrospect, I understood all that the minister and others in the church service had been implying. Because of our own class-based narrow mindedness, segments of the black population often didn't react to or care about racially biased abuses until one of our own—a black member of our socioeconomic class—had been victimized. Every city's black elite had one of these pivotal moments when an abuse reached into its own group and shook up an otherwise complacent community of professionals. In the spring of 1972, shortly before our visit there, Chicago's elite

Community had experienced its incident.

For years, ever since the ghettoization of blacks occurred on the south Side around the second decade of the 1900s, white Chicago police officers had been stopping and harassing blacks who dared venture east of Cottage Grove Avenue or north of Twenty-sixth Street, the early boundaries of the newly outlined black belt. However, it wasn't until two prominent black dentists, in two completely unrelated incidents, were jailed and harassed by the police that the black elite in the city (and else-where) became outraged.

In the spring of 1972, Dr. Herbert Odom was arrested after police noticed that one of the rear lights on his Cadillac was not working. The second arrest took place when an even more prominent dentist, Dr. Daniel Claiborne, suffered a severe stroke while driving along a South Side street. Dismissing his unconsciousness as intoxication by alcohol, Chicago police officers arrested Dr. Claiborne despite his obvious need for immediate medical attention. Instead of taking him to a hospital, they put him in jail, and he died shortly after the incident.

As the black elite read about these kinds of incidents in their local black weekly papers and in Jet, a weekly magazine, Published by Johnson Publications, that reports such incidents faithfully, they saw their quiet lives being disrupted even more as they ventured into affluent and peaceful white neighborhoods. My own parents saw this in the late 1960s one quiet afternoon when a police squad car attempted to take me and my eight-year-old brother off our residential street; the officer presumed that the red wagon my brother was pulling me in must have been stolen from a house in our white neighborhood.

Figure 23.
Johnson Publishing Company 2003

"Rich blacks don't start seeing the light about bigotry and police abuse until it starts happening to their own. It's not real to them when poor blacks are getting beaten up," says a South Side physician who knew Dr. Claiborne and recalled how the incident mobilized many of the professional blacks in Chicago. "A lot of us knew that poor blacks in the Ida B. Wells projects, Cabrini Green, and Robert Taylor Homes were being beaten up, but now Chicago Police were hitting too close to home. There was a reason why—years after integration—the U.S. Civil Rights Commission called Chicago the most residentially segregated city in America.

Since Chicago's city neighborhoods were more segregated than the neighborhoods of other cities, many wonder why so many black-owned enterprises succeeded there. In fact, many New Yorkers ask why New York's black population of the 1940s and 1950s—a larger and less con-fined community than Chicago's black South Side—was not producing black-owned businesses at a rate equal to that of Chicago. The explanation that many offer is surprising. Many black businessmen reason that Chicago's extreme segregation made it possible—or better yet, necessary—for blacks to build businesses that attracted undiluted black support. Black Harlemites supported white-owned establishments that populated most of Harlem and in other non-black neighborhoods where blacks lived and shopped.

And—using New York for a further comparison—because its black population of the 1930s and 1940s, for instance, was less ghettoized and was dispersed in many noncontiguous Manhattan, Brooklyn, and Bronx neighborhoods—Harlem, San Juan Hill, Greenwich Village, Brownsville, Ocean Hill, and the South Bronx, for example—black economic power was diluted. Chicago's blacks were ghettoized into one relatively easily defined area, and because of such boundaries—south of Twenty-sixth Street—black-owned and black-run businesses were able to fuel the community and flourish.

Truman Gibson Jr. and Maudelle Bousfield Evans [Principal of Wendell Phillips High School before Dr. Virginia Lewis], two insiders from the black belt, insist that the city changed a great deal during the decades they spent there. As black South Side residents, they saw Chicago in the 1930s become a leader in producing black congressmen. They saw Chicago in the 1940s become a community of black elites who fought amongst each other because of political party labels and patronage. And they saw Chicago after the 1950s become a town of more unified blacks who became equally outraged by the uniform mistreatment they faced under the Chicago political machine. In the 1960s and 1970s, they saw a Chicago that reluctantly opened up opportunities to upwardly mobile blacks. And in the 1980s, they saw Harold Washington, one of their own race and class, elected to the position of mayor, City of Chicago.

Although their fathers both grew up in the late 1800s, graduated from Harvard and Northwestern Medical School, and then became well-to-do businessmen while running the most powerful black-owned business in Chicago between the 1920s and 1950s, Gibson and Evans remember their privileged youth against a backdrop of a midwestern city that remained racially polarized longer than any other. It was a city that was run by a white elite that used restrictive covenants and other bizarre discriminatory laws to keep blacks in their place—on the South Side.

As adults, Gibson and Evans have seen much of the city's old bigotry erode. Always accomplished and successful, they and their colleagues have pushed farther north into neighborhoods and institutions their fathers never would have imagined. Gibson, a successful attorney and member of the Boule, laughs when his all-black chapter meets at the Union League Club downtown. "When I was a student going to the University of Chicago, both the school and the members of this club were part of the conservative leadership that worked to enforce restrictive covenants against blacks and keep us out of good neighborhoods and important networking clubs like this," explains Gibson, "but now we've rotten to see blacks head a lot of major institutions, including the Union League."

For Evans, a founding member of the Chicago Girl Friends who holds a master's degree in biology, the pivotal point was probably the week she and her husband, a retired magazine publisher who was also the nation's highest-ranking black advertising executive, moved into a duplex apartment on the sixty-fourth floor of the John Hancock Buliding on Chicago's Magnificent Mile.

17. Graham, Lawrence Otis [1999] Our Kind of People. New York: HarperCollins. pp. 185-187.

My father made the mistake of registering as a Republican in a community dominated by Democratic Party politics. Our next door neighbor, Mr. Jones, was the Republican Precinct Captain. My father thought that registering as a Republican only once, would satisfy Mr. Jones, and he could register as a Democrat for the next election. I happened to visit the Democratic Committeeman's office seeking employment, when I was told that they could not support my request because my father had registered as a Republican. I confronted my father and asked him to change his position as soon as possible, because he had been given poor advice. Mr. Jones must have heard the conversation, because he appeared, and walked me to the office of the Republican Committeeman. However, I never received a political appointment for a job that summer. What my father failed to understand is that the community that we lived in was similar to a plantation with a black master, William L. Dawson.

William L. Dawson

William Levi Dawson was born on this date in 1886. He was an African-American lawyer and politician. Born in Albany, Georgia he attended the public schools, graduating from Albany (Ga.) Normal School in 1905 and Fisk University, Nashville, Tenn., in 1909.

Dawson went to Kent College of Law (Chicago) and Northwestern University Law School. In World War I, he served overseas as a first lieutenant with the Three Hundred and Sixty-fifth Infantry 1917-1919. was admitted to the bar in 1920. He was the first African American to chair a regular House of Representatives committee. Dawson became one of Chicago's most influential politicians, serving as an elected representative and a political power broker in that city.

In this way he parallels the rising significance of African Americans in Democratic politics of the twentieth century. Three years after he graduated magna cum laude from Fisk University in 1912, Dawson moved to Chicago to study law at Northwestern University; once finished he entered into local politics. In 1942, after serving as alderman on the Chicago City Council, Dawson successfully ran for Congress, holding his seat until retiring in 1970.

Dawson spoke out about the poll tax, and was credited with defeating the Winstead Amendment, which would have allowed military personnel to choose whether or not they would serve in integrated units. In 1949, Dawson became chair of the House Committee on Expenditures in Executive Departments (later renamed the Committee on Government Operations), making him the first African American to chair a regular Congressional Committee.

In Chicago, where he was known As simply "The Man," Dawson developed a considerable power base by awarding political appointments to his allies. Similarly, President John F. Kennedy acknowledged Dawson's work in the 1960 campaign by offering him the Postmaster General's position. Dawson, however, turned the position down, preferring to remain in the House where he felt he could do the most good.

For all of the power he amassed, Dawson remained connected to his constituency. He returned to his district often and spent part of each day in his district office, visiting with constituents and working to solve their problems. He died in 1970.

18.http://wwwaaregistry.com/african_american_history/164/William L. Dawson_windy_C...11/25/2003\

THE RESURRECTION OF BRONZEVILLE

I was wishing my friend and neighbor, Tom Gray, former Amoco Corporation computer specialist, and presently the Administrator of Special Events for City Hall, a happy new year for 2004, when we entered into a serious discussion. Tom had invited me to an outdoor barbeque on 31st at Calumet in the heart of Bronzeville in 1984. Alderman, now Congressman, Bobby Rush, was a speaker, and many other friends, including the City Planner for the City of Chicago were present. Tom had purchased a home in the 31st block of Calumet and he was very excited about the expected gentrifying of Bronzeville. I imagined that there would be some improvement here or there, but nothing like the scope that is apparent in 2003.

I told Tom that a graystone on 35th at Indiana, where the Democratic Committeeman once lived was on the market for $450,000.00. It was located across the street from the former Williamson's Supermarket, and Clark's Poolroom. Tom told me that a house across the street from his in the 31st Street block of Calumet was sold for over $900,000.00. It occurred to me that if I had gone door to door in the entire Bronzeville community, I couldn't have collected $200,000.00 in the entire neighborhood, when I lived in that very historic setting.

Driving through the southside, which has been renamed the "fashionable south loop", one can only wonder at the change. Races of all complexions are moving south, replacing poorer black families, refurbishing homes at great expense, and moving in. The 35th street block of Prairie Avenue, where I lived, and attended Wendell Phillips High School, has many new town homes replacing vacant lots, older homes, and families.

The community surrounding King High School has been made over to the extent that friends who once lived there, drive through to admire the extreme changes. They tell others, and they make it a point to view the changes also. I was almost laughed out of a room, when I told friends that the new white neighbors were shopping at the Spot-Lite Market on 43rd at Lake Park. Earlier this year, Two blocks south of the Spot-Lite Market, several men were on trial for beating two men to death, after they lost control of their van, and crashed into a front porch killing one sitter, and wounding others.

Figure 24
Tom Gray

Tom Gray purchased a 95 tear old home in 1977. Six years, and $156,000.00 later, it became a 4,000 square-foot showplace. The once boarded up building was designed by Louis Sullivan, mentor of Frank Lloyd Wright. Tom Gray's project is typical of the type of renovation that is going on in the Gap area as he and other newcomers are investing hundreds of thousands of dollars into reviving the community.

In 1977, A group associated with the local Christ the Mediator Lutheran Church, formed to encourage newcomers, and provide them with information about available propertyand how the value of the homes had escalated over the years. Tom Gray, headed this organization, at its inception. They held seminars at the church, and told of the types of problems, prospective buyers might encounter. They also put homeowners in touch with contractors, who are familiar with working on old buildings.

19. The Amoco Torch. January/February 1985

Once a meeting place for neighborhood winos, Gray's home is now a showplace with a handsome stairway ascending from a marble foyer.

Designated a Chicago landmark in 1979, these English Tudor-style row houses one block from Gray's home were designed by renowned architect Frank Lloyd Wright and built in 1894.

Once a meeting place for neighborhood winos, Gray's home is now a showplace with a handsome stairway ascending from a marble foyer.

Designated a Chicago landmark in 1979, these English Tudor-style row houses one block from Gray's home were designed by renowned architect Frank Lloyd Wright and built in 1894.

A view of Gray's living room with its marble fireplace, bay window, 12-foot ceilings, and intricate shutters.

Gray relaxes in the family sitting room.

Left: A view of Gray's dining room complete with antique furniture.

Figures 25 And 26. The Tom Gray Residence In Bronzeville And English Tudor-style Row Houses One Block From Tom Gray's Home, Designed By Renowned Architech, Frank Lloyd Wright

The Bronzeville neighborhood is presently in a total state of rehabilitation. Its' transformation is obviously a "positive" for the city with the city organizations working together with the investment resources of private individuals, and speculators. The schools hope to be improved in the process, along with neighborhoods that were thought to be beyond the reach of moneylenders for reconstruction. There are some inhabitants who have chosen to remain in the community, but are having difficulty because the taxes on local property skyrocket, along with the value of upscale property in their neighborhood. The city has made some adjustments for those at the lower end of annual income scales. Others, who have resided in the neighborhood, who are not property owners, are having a difficult time finding new places to live, because the west side of Chicago is also undergoing the same type of change. Those Chicagoans, who have resided in public housing, are in the process of being relocated to surrounding suburbs, and others are lucky enough to resettle in the same neighborhood, or high-rise, from which they had been asked to leave at an earlier time.

I can only hope that the best outcome for all Chicagoans is in the near future.

SOMEONE ASKED GHANDI WHAT HE THOUGHT OF WESTERN CIVILIZATION: HE RESPONDED " I THINK IT WOULD BE A GOOD IDEA."

I have always thought that an educator should broaden his or her education by travel. With the improvement of my education in mind, I visited Hong Kong, Taiwan, and Canton, China, London, England, Monaco, Canne, Paris, Nice, and Marseilles, France, Athens, and Rhodes, Greece, Amsterdam, Holland, Naples, Pompei, and Rome, Italy, Instanbul, Turkey , Barcelona, Spain, Malta, Gibralta, Tunis, Tunisia, Rio de Janeiro, Brazil, Buenos Aires, Argentina, Mexico City, Cancun, and Acapulco, Mexico, Casablanca, and Marachese, Morroco, The Church of the Nazarene in Jerusalem, Israel, , Ho Chi Mihn City, Vietnam, Bangkok, Thailand, Honolulu, Hawaii, Toronto, Montreal, and Quebec City, Canada, and the islands of Barbados, Aruba, in the Netherlands Antilles, Nassau, Freeport, St. Lucia, Martinique, St. Thomas, et al,

BRIEF BIO

Dr. Robert D. Brazil was Principal of Francis Parker High School for three years, before beginning his tenure of sixteen years as principal of Sullivan High. He has worked for the U.S. Department of Justice, Instructor at the National College of Education, and Northern Illinois University, Assistant Professor, University of Illinois, and Director of the Paideia Institute of Hyde Park. Dr. Brazil received his degrees from Chicago Teachers College, De Paul University, and the University of Illinois, Urbana- Champaign, with advanced graduate studies at Northwestern University, St. John's College, Santa Fe, New Mexico, and the University of Oxford, England. He is author of <u>The Engineering of the Paideia Proposal 1988,</u> and <u>A Covenant for Change 1990,</u> both published by the University of Illinois Press. <u>His latest work, Beyond This place, There be Dragons</u>, 2000, described the Paideia approach to learning in schools on probation. The foreword was written by Chicago Public School C.E.O., Paul Vallas. www.firstbooks.com

Dr. Brazil has accumulated numerous awards for Sullivan High School, including every one offered by the City of Chicago, The Chicago Board of Education, and the Rogers Park Community Council for Anti-Vandalism and Beautification. Other awards for Sullivan have come from the Illinois Alliance of Essential Schools, Fel- Pro Corporation , The Field Foundation, IBM, The Carnegie Foundation, The Amoco Foundation, The Joyce Foundation, The Whitman Foundation, The Joyce and Searles Foundations, The W. Alton Jones Foundation , and the John D. and Catherine T. Mac Arthur Foundation.

Ten teachers under his stewardship have been named winners of the Blum- Kovler Outstanding Teacher Award, presented annually at the University of Chicago. Visitors from England to Australia to Alaska, and most of the contiguous states have come to view the implementation of the Paideia Proposal, and the Coalition of Essential Schools Programs championed by Mortimer J. Adler at the Institute for Philosophical Research, and Ted Sizer at Brown University, respectively. Dr. Brazil worked as an associate of Dr. Mortimer Adler at the Institute for Philosophical Research, until Dr. Adler retired, and moved to San Mateo, California.

Dr. Brazil has won many awards himself. He was named outstanding Principal in District Two, Outstanding Secondary Principal in

Chicago by the Citizens Schools Committee, Whitman Foundation Awardee for Outstanding Principal in Chicago, and in 1992 received the "Those Who Excel Award" from State Superintendent of Schools, Robert Leininger. He directs the Staff Development of many Paideia Schools in Chicago, as it relates to The Paideia Proposal, and in other cities. He also works as a consultant for the Chicago Public Schools, and facilitator for Immersion Retreats at Lake Geneva, Wisconsin, and Graduate Institutes at St. John's College, Santa Fe, New Mexico and The University of Oxford, England. Dr. Brazil has served as Probation Manager for two Chicago Public High Schools and one Chicago Elementary School.

NOTES

1. Bronzeville. Copyright 2003 City of Chicago Department of Planning and Development, Landmarks Division http://www.ci.chi.il.us/landmarks/B/BlackMet.html

2. Ida B. Wells. www.chipub.org/001hwcl/gisnotableafam.html

3. William G. Stratton. http://www.legis.state.il.us/legislation/legisnet92/hrgroups/hr/920hr0113LV.html

4. General Benjamin O. Davis. http://www.af.mil/bios/bio_5173.shtml

5. The Victory Monument. Copyright 2003 City of Chicago Department of Planning and Development, Landmarks Division. http://www.ci.chi.il.us/Landmarks/V/Victory.html

6. Supreme Liberty Life Insurance Building. Black Metropolis-Bronzeville Historic District. Copyright 2003 City of Chicago Department of Planning and Development, Landmarks Division.

    http://www.ci.chi.il.us/Landmarks/S/Supreme.html

7. EarlB.Dickerson.

    http://www.chipublib.org/001hwlc/gisnotableafam.html

8. The Wabash YMCA Copyright 2003 City of Chicago Department of Planning and Development, Landmarks Division.

    http://www.ci.chi.il.us/LANDMARKS/w/wABASH YMCA.html

9. The Eighth Regiment Armory. Copyright 2003 City of Chicago

    Department of Planning and Development, Landmarks Division

    http://www.ci.chi.il.us/Landmarks/E/EighthRegiment.html

10 THE ART INSTITUTE OF CHICAGO. HTTP://WWW.ARTIC.EDU

11 The Chicago Public Library's Harold Washingon Library Center, 400 South State Street.History of the Chicago Public library: Windows of Our Past http://www.chipublib.org

12 <u>Last of the " Old School" Educators</u>, Carl Boyd. Advice Media Publications 2001

13 http://www.depaul.edu.

14 www.uiuc.edu/

15 Copy right 2003 City of Chicago Department of Planning anddevelopment, Landmarks Division.

http://www.ci.chi.il.us/Landmarks/D/Defender.html

16 Grossman, James R.[1989]. Land of Hope Chicago, Black Southerners, and the Great Migration. Chicago:University of Chicago Press. "Home People and Old Settlers" PP. 123-130.

17. Graham, Lawrence Otis [1989] Our Kind of People.

Chicago: University of Chicago Press. pp. 185-187.

18 William L. Dawson. http://wwwaaregistry.com/african_american_history/1 64/William

19 *The Amoco Torch. January/February 1985*

Printed in the United States
44712LVS00005B/3